WEST OF KABUL,
EAST OF NEW YORK

WEST OF KABUL, EAST OF NEW YORK

·

AN AFGHAN AMERICAN STORY

·

TAMIM ANSARY

FARRAR, STRAUS AND GIROUX

NEW YORK

·

Farrar, Straus and Giroux
19 Union Square West, New York 10003

Copyright © 2002 by Tamim Ansary
All rights reserved
Distributed in Canada by Douglas & McIntyre Ltd.
Printed in the United States of America
First edition, 2002

A portion of the chapter "The Convert" was originally published, in slightly different form, in Chanteh *magazine as "Killing the Lamb."*

ISBN: 0-374-28757-0
Library of Congress Control Number: 2002102958

Designed by Abby Kagan

www.fsgbooks.com

1   3   5   7   9   10   8   6   4   2

For my children, Jessamyn and Elina

WEST OF KABUL,
EAST OF NEW YORK

PROLOGUE

FOR MANY LONG YEARS, my siblings and I thought we were the only Afghans in America. When I introduced myself to people, they'd say, "Interesting name. Where are you from?" When I said Afghanistan, I could feel myself changing, not unpleasantly, into a curiosity. Few knew where Afghanistan was, and some were amazed to learn it existed at all. Once, in a college gym class, a coach found my free-throw shooting form humorous. "Where have you been all your life," he guffawed, "*Afghanistan?*" When I said yes, he was taken aback: he thought Afghanistan was just an expression, like ultima Thule, meaning "off the map."

The Soviet invasion put Afghanistan on the map, but it didn't last. By the summer of 2001, a new acquaintance could say to me, "Afghanistan, huh? I never would have guessed you're from Africa."

That all changed on September 11, 2001. Suddenly, everywhere I went, strangers were talking about Kandahar and Kunduz and Mazar-i-Sharif. On September 12, the abrupt notoriety of Afghanistan triggered a volcanic moment in my own small life.

I was driving around San Francisco that day, listening to talk radio. My mind was chattering to itself about errands and deadlines, generating mental static to screen me off from my underlying emotions, the turmoil and dread. On the radio, a woman caller was making a tearful, ineffective case against going to war over the terrorist attacks in New York and Washington. The talk-show host derided her. A man called in to say that the enemy was not just Afghanistan but people like that previous caller as well. The talk-show host said thoughtfully, "You're making a lot of sense, sir."

The next caller elaborated on what should be done to Afghanistan: "Nuke that place. Those people have to learn. Put a fence around it! Cut them off from medicine! From food! Make those people starve!"

More than thirty-five years had passed since I had seen Afghanistan, but the ghosts were still inside me, and as I listened to that apoplectically enraged talk on the radio, those ghosts stirred to life. I saw my grandmother K'koh, elfin soul of the Ansary family. Oh, she died long ago, but in my mind she died again that day, as I pictured the rainfall of bombs that would be coming. And I saw my father, the man who wouldn't, or couldn't, leave when the Soviets

4

put the country in a clamp. He was long gone, too, but if he'd lived, he would be in Kabul now, an eighty-three-year-old man, in rags on the streets, his ribs showing, one of the many who would be starving when the fence was flung up around our land.

I didn't begrudge those callers their rage, but I felt a bewilderment deeper than shock. No one seemed to know how pitifully harmless Afghans were, strong contenders for the Poorest People on Earth award, overrun by the world's most hardened criminals, and now, it seemed, marked out to suffer for the crimes of their torturers.

I wanted to call that talk show, but when I came home, I felt too shy. I'd never spoken to the media at any level. So I went downstairs to my office and wrote an e-mail to a few of my friends. I poured out to them what I would have said to the public if I could have mustered the courage to call that talk show. The moment I clicked on SEND, I felt infinitesimally better.

Later that day, some of the people on my list asked if they could pass my note on to their friends, and I said, "Sure," thinking, Wow, with luck, I might reach fifty or sixty people.

That night, I logged on to my server and found a hundred e-mails in my in-box, mostly from strangers responding to the message I'd hammered out earlier. It boggled my mind. The power of the Internet! I had reached . . . hundreds.

The next day, I realized something bigger was rising

under me. At noon I got a call from my old friend Nick Allen, whom I hadn't seen in fifteen years. Somehow, he'd received the e-mail and had felt moved to track me down and say hi.

An hour later, I heard from Erik Nalder, the son of an American engineer, whom I had last seen in Afghanistan thirty-eight years ago. He'd received my e-mail—I couldn't imagine how—and had felt moved to track me down and say hi.

Then the phone rang again. A caller from Chicago. A hesitant voice. "My name is Charles Sherman. . . ." Did I know this guy? "I got your e-mail. . . ." I couldn't place him. "You don't know me," he said.

"Then how did you get my number?"

"I looked you up on the Internet—anyone can get your number. . . . I just wanted to tell you that . . . your e-mail made a lot of sense to me."

I thanked him and hung up, but my heart was pounding. Strangers were reading my e-mail, and anyone could get my phone number. What if the next caller said, "Hi, I'm with the Taliban"? What if Al Qaeda knocked on the door? How long before some hysterical racist sent a brick through my window?

I wanted to cancel my e-mail. "I've reached enough people, thank you; that will be all." But it was too late. I couldn't withdraw the e-mail. I couldn't issue corrections, amendments, or follow-ups. My e-mail spread like a virus throughout the United States and across the world. My e-mail accounts overflowed with responses, and the servers had to start deleting messages I had not read. Radio stations started calling—then newspapers—then TV. By the fourth day, I found myself putting *World News Tonight* on hold to take a call from Oprah's people—inconceivable! I have no idea how many people received the e-mail ultimately. A radio station in South Africa claimed it reached 250,000 people in that country alone. Worldwide, I have to guess, it reached millions—within a week.*

What had I written? I wondered. Why the response? I barely had time to ponder these bewildering questions. The media seized on me as a pundit. The questions came at me like hornets pouring out of a nest, and all I could do was swing at them. From those first few insane weeks, I only remember Charlie Rose's skeptical face looming toward me with the question, "But Tamim . . . can you really compare the Taliban to *Nazis?*"

I tried to tell him about that guy I'd met in Turkey, the one in the pin-striped suit who had wanted to convert me to his brand of Islam, and the horror that had filled me as I read his literature afterward, but my long-winded digression wasn't appropriate for that or any TV show. I stumbled out of the studio, my mind reeling. What *did* I mean? The words I had used in that e-mail were so brutal. The Taliban, I had written, are a

---

*The text of the e-mail appears on pages 289–292.

CULT
of *IGNORANT*
PSYCHOTICS.
When you think *BIN LADEN*, think
HITLER.

I never would have used such language if I'd thought millions of people were listening. I'm sure I would have measured my language more carefully. But in that case, probably no one would have listened. And had I misspoken? Would I now renounce my words? I decided the answer was no.

Two weeks later, my cousin's wife, Shafiqa, called to tell me there was going to be a memorial service for Ahmed Shah Massoud that night, complete with speeches, videotapes, posters, and more speeches. I should come.

Massoud was the last credible anti-Taliban leader in Afghanistan, the man who put together the Northern Alliance, a towering figure, assassinated by Arab suicide bombers two days before the attacks on the World Trade Center. I admired Massoud, and his assassination disheartened me, but I was just too spent to go to his memorial service. "I need to rest," I pleaded.

Shafiqa was silent for a moment. Then she said, "Listen, Tamim, we are all proud of what you have done. You have written a letter. That's good. But Massoud slept with only a stone for a pillow for twenty-three years. He scarcely knew the names of his children, because he would not set down the burden of liberating our country. I think he was tired at times, too. I think you should be at his memorial service."

I hung my head in shame and said I would be there.

The following week, a representative of the Northern Alliance phoned me. "You have the ear of the American media. You know how to say things. We know what things must be said. Let us work together. From now on, you must be the spokesman."

"The spokesman? For what? For whom?"

"For our cause. For our country."

I could feel my ears shutting down and my eyes looking for the back door. Was Afghanistan really my country?

Dear reader, let me pause to introduce myself properly. Yes, I was born and raised in Afghanistan, and I know Islam intimately, from the inside, in my very soul. Yes, I learned to say my prayers from my Afghan grandmother; yes, I know the flavor of sundown on the first day of Ramadan, when you're on the porch with the people you love, waiting for the cannon that will mark the moment when a white thread can no longer be distinguished from a black one and you can put the day's first sweet date in your mouth.

But my mother was American, and not just any American, but a secular one to the max, and a feminist back when there hardly *was* such a thing—the daughter of an immigrant labor agitator in Chicago who would have been a Communist if only he could have accepted orders from anyone but his own conscience. And I moved to America at age sixteen, and graduated from Reed College, and grew my hair down to my waist, and missed Woodstock by minutes, and revered Bob Dylan back when his voice still worked. I made a career in educational publishing, and if you have children, they have probably used some product I have edited or written. I am an American.

How could I be an adequate spokesman for Afghanistan or for Muslims?

"Look, I have nothing to tell people but my own small story," I told the fellow from the Northern Alliance. "Maybe I can help Americans see that Afghans are just human beings like anyone else. That's about all I can do."

"That is important, too," he said, his voice softened by anxiety and despair.

In the weeks that followed, however, the media kept punching through to me, and I kept answering their questions. It turned out that I did have plenty to say about Afghanistan, Islam, and fundamentalism, because I have been pondering these issues all my life—the dissonance between the world I am living in now and the world I left behind, a world that is lost to me. And as I kept talking, it struck me that I was not the only one who had lost a world. There was a lot of loss going around. Perhaps it wasn't really nostalgia for the seventh century that was fueling all this militancy. Perhaps it was nostalgia for a world that existed much more recently, traces of which still linger in the social memory of the Islamic world. Lots of people have parents, or grandparents, or at least great-grandparents who grew up in that world. Some people even know that world personally, because they were born in it. I am one of those people.

PART ONE

.

The Lost World

VILLAGES AND COMPOUNDS

IN 1948, WHEN I WAS BORN, most of Afghanistan might as well have been living in Neolithic times. It was a world of walled villages, each one inhabited by a few large families, themselves linked in countless ways through intermarriages stretching into the dim historical memories of the eldest elders. These villages had no cars, no carts even, no wheeled vehicles at all; no stores, no shops, no electricity, no postal service, and no media except rumors, storytelling, and the word of travelers passing through. Virtually all the men were farmers. Virtually all the women ran the households and raised the children. Virtually all boys grew up to be like their fathers and all girls like their mothers. The broad patterns of life never changed, never had as far as any living generation could remember, and presumably never would. People lived pretty much as they had eight thousand years ago.

That was the countryside. The big cities, such as Kandahar and Mazar-i-Sharif, were living in the fifteenth century or so. And the biggest city, Kabul, where my family lived, had made it to the twentieth century, but just barely. Cars were few, roads were unpaved, and public transportation consisted mostly of *gadis*—horse-drawn two-wheeled carriages. Electricity was scarce, too. Most of us used kerosene lanterns at night. There was no running water. We all had wells. There was no garbage service. We didn't produce any garbage. Hundreds of thousands of people lived in the city, but the houses had no numbers and the streets had no names. If you didn't know where you were going, you probably had no business going there. A postal service existed, but it didn't deliver to private homes unless the mailman felt like it, and he felt like it only if he knew you or had heard of you. Yet even with hundreds of thousands of people in the city, the postman very possibly had heard of you. Oh, not *you* in particular; you were just a leaf, a bud. He'd know the branch, the trunk, the tree itself: your people.

Everybody in the city lived in a compound, a yard surrounded by walls that divided the world into a public and a private realm. That's the main fact I want to get across about the lost world I grew up in: It was not divided into a men's world and a women's world; the division was between public and private. Visitors never really knew us, because they never saw the hidden world inside our compounds. Those who came from the West didn't even know our private universe existed, or that life inside it was warm and sweet. And in a way, we Afghans didn't know we had this realm either, because we didn't know it was possible not to have it.

In the compounds, people spent all their time with the group. As far as I can tell, none of my Afghan relatives was ever alone or ever wanted to be. And that's so different from my life today, here in the West. Because I write for a living, I spend most of my waking hours alone in my basement office. Oh, I jog, do errands, see people I know—but mostly, it's just a man and his thoughts in a blur of urban landscape. If I'm too much with other people, I need to balance it with some downtime. Most of the people I know are like this. We need solitude, because when we're alone, we're free from obligations, we don't need to put on a show, and we can hear our own thoughts.

My Afghan relatives achieved this same state by being with one another. Being at home with the group gave them the satisfactions we associate with solitude—ease, comfort, and the freedom to let down one's guard. The reason for this is hard to convey, but I'm going to try. Namely, our group self was just as real as our individual selves, perhaps more so.

I don't know what term properly applies to this type of group. *Family* doesn't cover it. Even *extended family* feels too small. *Tribe,* however, is too big. I'm inclined to hijack the term *clan* from anthropology, although even that is not quite right, because the type of group I'm talking about was not a formal entity, had no organization, no name, no recognized chief, and no exact boundaries. It was more like a loose network of extended families tied together by a mutual sense of having descended from a great someone in the past—or a string of great someones.

Our group, for example, looked back to Sa'aduddin, a landowner who lived in the nineteenth century and wrote mystical poetry under the pen name Shuri Ishq— "Turmoil of Love." He was my great-great-grandfather. Of course, Americans too might have a sense of identity based on a famous ancestor, but the Afghan experience differs from the American one, because Afghans prefer to marry their relatives. In America, hardly anyone actually seeks to date their kin, but in Afghanistan, the ideal marriage is between first cousins. Therefore, in Afghanistan, the lines of descent from an important man tend to keep curling back toward the center, endlessly weaving a coherent entity through intermarriage. And that's the entity I'll call a "clan" from now on, because "network of extended families descended from a great someone" is too cumbersome.

We tended to feel more at home with others of our own large group than we did with strangers, and the Afghan tradition of living in compounds deepened this tendency. Once we stepped into one of our compounds in those days, each of us had a different name from the one we used outside. These names were called *luqubs* and were all constructed of the same few words—*flower, lion, sugar, lord, lady, sweet,* and so on, combined with *uncle, aunt, papa, mama,* and the like. My mother's name, for example, was Khanim Gul, meaning "Lady Flower."

In a compound, the old, young, and middle-aged—

men, women, girls, and boys—all shared the same space. Living quarters weren't divided into your space and his space and my space. People didn't have places to keep their possessions—few, in fact, had much in the way of possessions: It wasn't a thing-centered world. By day, thin mattresses arranged along the perimeters of the rooms served as furniture. At night, blankets were pulled out of closets and those same mattresses were rearranged in the center of the floor as beds.

At mealtime, any room could become the dining room. A tablecloth would be spread on the floor. Everyone would wash their hands thoroughly and eat with them from a common platter, packed together so tightly around the food on the tablecloth that their oneness was a physical experience, a circle of people who were all touching.

Instead of television, we had genealogy. The elders, the white-headed ones, spent endless hours with one another or with us youngsters, tracing connections. So-and-so married so-and-so, and then their progeny got sorted into these other branches through marriage, so actually your cousin Saliq is your second cousin through Sweet Daddy— and so on. It might not sound exciting, but remember that genealogy was the warp and family stories the woof of the fabric that made us one entity.

We didn't spend much time pondering Islam. We didn't have to. Islam permeated the life of the compound like the custard that binds a casserole together, hardly separable from ordinary daily life. Five times a day, some of us did our ablutions and moved into the prayer ritual, one by one, at our own pace. Prayer divided a day into five parts and gave a sort of rhythm to the household, like breathing in, holding for quiet, and then breathing out, releasing back into noise and activity. There was no Ministry of Vice and Virtue. No one was under the gun to pray; it was not an obligation, just a custom and a way of life. At prayer call, those who didn't pray lowered their speaking voices out of respect for those who did, and we youngsters learned not to be doing our naughtiness near a person who was praying, so that we wouldn't embarrass them by seeing the undignified sight they presented when they got on their hands and knees and touched their forehead to the floor.

In winter, the intervals were shorter; in summer, longer. Some men went to the mosque on Fridays, but that wasn't the locus of Islam in old Afghanistan: It was everywhere. The rhythm of prayer suffused the city, the whole society, all the villages, all the world, as far as we were aware. With so many people praying at once, at home, in the court-yards, in public buildings, five times daily, prayer became the respiration of a whole society calming down at intervals in a rhythm set not by any clock but by the light of nature.

Now let me place my family in this scene. We were an exception of sorts, because my mother was American. She met my father in Chicago, where the Afghan government had sent him to acquire Western knowledge. My father,

Amanuddin, was the fourth of five brothers and the second of the five to be sent abroad for such an education. He learned to read and write from the village mullah and entered the government school as a sixth grader, and it was just about then that the royal family decided Afghanistan needed Western know-how. My father's elder brother Najmuddin got one of the first of the government scholarships to a university in the West, but the year after he left, a terrible event cut the scholarship program short, an event that my father witnessed. Indeed, this event almost cost my father his life.

He was in seventh grade at the time. He and other worthy students from several Kabul high schools had been called to the palace for an awards ceremony, during which one of my father's classmates stepped out of the ranks and shot the monarch dead. This king, Nadir Shah, a stern, skinny figure with small round spectacles, had ruled for only a few years. Although his clan had owned the throne for some 150 years, his particular family had been an outlying branch until the third Afghan-British war, from which Nadir emerged as a war hero. A few years later, a bandit known as "the Water-Carrier's Son" led a revolt against the monarchy and drove King Amanullah out of the country. Nadir, however, took the field and routed the rebels. But instead of handing the throne back to Amanullah, he claimed it for himself. Some families in the royal clan regarded Nadir as a usurper. The boy who killed him belonged to one of these.

As soon as the bodyguards saw the king fall, they locked

the courtyard gates and prepared to shoot down all the students. But the king's son, the teenaged prince Zahir Shah, who had flung himself upon his father's warm corpse in shock and grief, had the presence of mind—and humanity—to take command and order the guards to hold their fire. My father owed his life to that prince, and I guess I do, too, indirectly. Perhaps this is why I have always felt such affection and respect for Zahir Shah, who was king of Afghanistan throughout my years there, the same king who was called out of exile after the Taliban collapsed, to preside over his country as a symbol of unity.

My father was one of five students sent to the United States the first year the scholarship program was resumed. He got his bachelor's degree from the University of Illinois and then studied at Stanford for a couple of weeks, but when he tried to find housing on the West Coast, landlords slammed their doors on him, snarling, "We don't rent to Japs!" This was during World War II, and my father's Mongolian blood showed somewhat in his features.

This contempt for his bloodline must have shocked him. In Afghanistan, no matter what reversals he might suffer or how low he might sink, one distinction could never be taken away from him—his bloodline. He was an Ansary, descended from one of those families in seventh-century Arabia who helped the Prophet Muhammad escape from Mecca to Medina. The Arabic word *ansar* means "helper," and descendants of those families have been known ever since as Ansarys.

Having encountered no racism in the Midwest, my father returned to the University of Chicago to pursue his Ph.D. in education. He lived in a boardinghouse with his hometown buddies, Shalizi, Taraki, Kayeum, and Asghar.

Downstairs in that same boardinghouse lived a shy first-generation Finnish-American girl named Terttu Palm: brown sausage-curl bangs, plump cheeks, a Clara Bow mouth, and the modest clothes of a girl who didn't consider herself pretty. She had grown up in the Finnish community of Chicago, speaking nothing but Finnish until she went to school, and even then her social world remained mainly Finnish, with a smattering of Russian in the mix. As a teenager, her idea of fun was attending dances at the Finnish community hall, where she waltzed and fox-trotted with Finnish boys (although I get the impression that she was mostly a wallflower, alas). Her dreamboats were never the athletes or the fast-talking boys who smoked and drank, but the boys who could trip the light fantastic.

She had just finished teachers college and was living on her own for the first time, free from the shadow of her domineering father, supporting herself as an elementary school teacher and hungering for life, when my father moved in upstairs. She idolized artists, bohemians, and all things exotic, and the Afghan boys attracted her like honey. She told me once that she didn't single out my father; she just wanted one of those Afghan boys, she didn't know which one.

My father looked like a skinny Gregory Peck, with a touch of the Mongolian horseman in his features. Stylish

in his wide suits, big ties, and snazzy hats, he had a devil-
may-care, artiste air about him. But he really emerged
from the pack when my mother discovered that he could
tango. The next few chapters of my parents' story are
shrouded in mist, and when the fog lifts, they're married.

Their wedding took place in the sixth year of my father's American adventure, and it got him in trouble. Before he left Afghanistan, he had signed a contract not to
marry a foreigner, an act already prohibited by the Afghan
constitution. As soon as he married my mother, the government recalled him, cutting his education short.

Afghanistan shocked my mother deeply at first. She did
a lot of crying that first year. She could not be reconciled to
living only in the world behind the walls. She wanted to go
home—but not without my father.

The royal government wanted her to go home, too—
but not with my father, whom they had spent a fortune educating. They ordered my father to send her back, but the
Ansarys got together and decided they could not let outsiders dictate to them in this matter of their womenfolk, so
they defied the royal family's order. I'm not sure what my
mother thought about this bravery on her behalf, since
she was longing to leave Afghanistan, but in any case, she
stayed.

With my grandmother leading the way, the family took
her in as the Permanent Guest, always to be honored,
loved, and cared for. Afghan society settled on treating her
as an exception to the rules of gender: She was considered
neither female nor male, but American. She never wore a

chad'ri (the body-length veil now commonly known as the *burqa*), and she soon began to work outside the compound. The government had just started the country's first girls' school, and my mother set about teaching Afghan girls to speak English. Since the role of teacher was an honored, almost sacred one in Afghan society, she carved a place for herself as "teacher-sir" to a generation of women.

I have to say that in the Afghan context, the government cut her a lot of slack. Once, she flunked a couple of girls in her class. The principal came to her, shocked and concerned, and said, "You can't fail those girls; they're high up in the royal family."

My mother replied sassily, "Well, in that case, I don't need to teach the class. Just tell me the rank of each student, so I can give her the appropriate grade, and we can all go home."

My father came in afterward to settle the ruffled feathers and smooth things over. I imagine he did a lot of that. He was a patient man, quietly humorous, prone to sudden enthusiasms, but usually distracted by ideas going on in his mind—much the same impression my children have of me, I think, except for the part about patience. He liked to putter in his elaborate garden far more than he did mixing it up in the rough-and-tumble of political life. His passion was literature, and he wrote poetry. So did all my uncles, but my father went a little further down this road, perhaps, since he taught literature at the brand-new Kabul University and eventually served as dean of that college.

It took him a few years to get his career started. The

government punished him at first for marrying a foreigner by refusing to employ him in any official capacity. But then the four other scholarship students in his class came back, and three of them brought home foreign wives (they cannily put off marrying their girlfriends until they had gotten their doctorates). The government gave up, forgave them all, amended the constitution, and gave my father his first teaching post.

Around that time, a new quarter of the city was opened to development, and a lottery was held for the right to buy parcels there. By some amazing coincidence, as my mother put it thirty years later, all four of the men with foreign wives won that lottery. The words were halfway out of her mouth before she realized that coincidence probably had nothing to do with it.

My sister Rebecca was born in 1946, and I came along two years later. Like my mother, we had a special place in the clan. We were right at the heart of it, although contained somewhat in the nuclear household my mother maintained within the Ansary social universe. At home, we didn't sit on the floor like other Ansarys; we had tables and chairs. We ate odd things like spaghetti, and we did so with silverware, not our hands. So when dining with other branches of the clan, we came in for some affectionate jesting, because eating with one's hand is, in fact, a refined and difficult skill, and we couldn't do it very well.

Rebecca and I shared a bedroom, and I have a cellular memory of our whispering together after the lights went out. When she fell asleep and left me alone in the dark, three feet away, I sometimes saw monsters on my eyelids and had to scream and wake her up. She took care of me like a peppery, pint-sized mommy, and between us, there was never any question about who was boss. And I liked it that way. She was our envoy to the adult world, marching out there to get the information we needed to know and then bringing it back to share with me. Apparently, we could communicate with each other before I could officially talk. I believe that early on I didn't have a clear sense of where I ended and she began. I'm told that if I was ever given candy, I automatically saved half for her. "What a sweet, unselfish boy," grown-ups said. But really I was only saving half the candy for my other mouth. Nothing unselfish about it, once you knew who the self was.

My mother stocked her nest as best she could with American items, which included canned foods, cocoa, classical music records, and books. One spring, when I was five or six, my sister taught me the English alphabet. By that fall, when my mother sat down to teach me phonics, I could already read every word in the third-grade reader except *sugar* and *enough*. I think I learned to read because I had such a hunger for stories. My cousins drank their fill of these from my grandmother and other family storytellers, but since Rebecca and I lived somewhat separately from the others, I had to make up the deficiency with books.

Soon, in addition to Afghanistan, I had a rich, imaginary, English-speaking world to live in. For a time, the grown-ups nicknamed me "Professor."

Our compound at the edge of the city was pretty typical for progressive Afghans of our social status in that day: an acre or so surrounded by a mud-brick wall about nine feet high, which kept strangers from peeking in on us and kept us from looking out, too, at ground level anyway. In the most traditional compounds, the buildings were attached to the perimeter walls, and these walls and buildings surrounded and protected an inner courtyard. Each compound had a front room for entertaining male visitors unrelated to the family. The visitors could be brought to this room without giving them any glimpse of the inner courtyard, the private world. In our compound, however, the main house was in the middle of the yard, because we were moving away from this preoccupation with keeping our women hidden from strangers.

We did, however, have buildings along our perimeter walls. A long row of rooms lined one outer wall, and each of them opened directly onto the yard—the outhouse, storerooms for extra bedding, wood and coal, onions and potatoes (which we kept buried in mounds of soil for freshness).

There were other buildings as well, all made of sun-baked brick. We had a sizable separate one-room building for any poor relation who might be living with us at any given time (and there was almost always someone). We had a two-room suite with its own little kitchen—a room with a smoke hole and a fire pit—where a succession of families unrelated to us lived. They were our *kinar-nisheen,* "those who dwelt in our corners." They were like vassals in a feudal system, poor people who depended on my father's patronage. As often as not, the father had some job of his own out in the world, but the wife and older children worked for us.

Although not strictly traditional, our compound was still a world apart. From the strawberry patch at the center of our yard, I could see nothing beyond the walls except mountains and sky—far to the south, the Safid Mountains, a jagged row of broken teeth, snowcapped all year round, the whites as sharp against the blue rocks as if etched with a needle point, a testament to the purity of Kabul's (then) unpolluted air. To the east, looming hulks spilled in from two directions, pinching the city almost in half. The Kabul River cut a narrow notch through this "Lion's Gate Mountain," and beyond the notch lay the busy chaos of downtown. Our side was mostly residential, and closer to us was a rock that looked like an enormous dinosaur—so close that its shadow blanketed our yard at certain hours, with Kabul University nestled between its flanks.

Our compound had two doors. One opened onto a plain, where boys from around the city came to fly their kites on Fridays and bands of nomads camped with their sheep, camels, and dogs. The other door opened onto an alley that wound among thirty or forty compounds before reaching a main thoroughfare. In that alley, we boys from the various compounds would play soccer and a form of cricket. Our bat was a stick carved from a tree branch, and our ball was a wad of rags wrapped in twine.

This alley, a dirt lane without pavement or sidewalks, was flanked by two continuous nine- or ten-foot-high adobe walls, which were punctuated by doors, each one decorative and unique.

Much of urban and even village Afghanistan had the narrow, hemmed-in feeling of this lane. Everything that made life worth living was private, and the splendid secret was there behind every door along that lane, behind every compound wall. The Kayeums lived about eight doors down from ours, and if you made it into the privacy of their compound, voilà—cherry blossoms, vegetables, flowering acacia trees, family, relatives, and retainers—just like ours. The same was true of both Shalizi's compound and Taraki's.

We knew these compounds very well, because Shalizi, Kayeum, and Taraki were three of the four men who had gone to America with my father, and all had foreign wives. The Kayeums were especially close to us because my father and Kayeum were best friends, and Kayeum and his wife, Joan, had five children, including Rona, a girl about my age. The Kayeum children were almost like siblings to Rebecca and me.

As a little boy, I never felt hemmed in by our compound walls. To me, the compound felt like a universe. At age five, I was still discovering places in it I had never seen. Besides, ours was just one of several compounds in our family network. Ansarys had other compounds in the city, each one anchored by a different patriarch. Not only was my father one of five brothers but my grandfather had four wives, so there were various half brothers kicking around. Each compound had its core of adults, but for the youngsters, the boundaries were somewhat fluid. If you went to another of the compounds for the day, you did not necessarily go home with your parents that night; you might stay on. It didn't really matter so much, here or there: It was like an American's choosing between the dining room and the family room in his own home.

In short, the many compounds of a clan like ours formed a sort of secret urban village. Women lived freely within the compounds, but they wore veils and traveled with male escorts to get from one compound to another. And each of these secret villages was connected to an actual village outside the city, in the nearby countryside, a village that felt like the soul of the extended family network. Going back to the ancestral village meant going home to a warmth and belonging that today, in my basement office in San Francisco, I can only imagine.

In this Afghanistan, this lost world, no one left the home village, or wanted to, and the concept of "dysfunctional family" had no meaning. Oh, quarrels and disagreements abounded, and they were never really buried; they were hashed and rehashed till they had been thoroughly mulched into the clan soil.

THE ANSARY NETWORK

W E ANSARYS HAILED from the village of Deh Yahya, ten or twenty miles outside the city of Kabul, itself a colony extended from another village about forty miles farther out. For several generations now, we had been creeping toward Kabul. In the city, Ansary Central was the compound anchored by my second-eldest uncle, a round-faced, soft-skinned, stern, bespectacled, five-foot-tall asthmatic by the name of Najmuddin. In my earliest memories, he was probably in his late forties. When he shook hands, he just placed his small hand in yours like a warm, boneless fish and let you do all the gripping and shaking. He liked to play chess, but if he began to lose, he would contrive to knock the chessboard over by accident.

He rarely ventured out of his yard, for fear that he might be struck by a bus or trampled by a donkey, and even in the compound he didn't like to stand up, for fear that he might fall down. Children, with their anarchic energy, damn near panicked him. He was a bachelor all his life—until his last year, when he fell in love, got married, got disillusioned, got divorced, and died, all within six months.

Najmuddin ruled our Ansary clan like a little Napoléon. Oh, he didn't have a title. Let me emphasize again, the clan, as I call it, was not a formal entity. My uncle didn't win an election. It's just that his brothers kowtowed to him, his mother protected him, and we children walked in fear of him. No one opposed his whims. In the family, we called him Khan Kaka, which means "Lordly Uncle." (Just for the record, the other four brothers were nicknamed "Dear Father," "Lion Father," "Discussion Leader Uncle"—my father—and the youngest, "Flower Uncle.")

Khan Kaka enjoyed considerable prestige in the wider world, as well as in our family. The city of Kabul respected him for his intellectual prowess solely because of his powers of conversation, as far as I could tell. His public room functioned as a salon, packed every day with people who stopped by to pay court to him, to marvel at his wit, to ponder his theories, or just to drink in his thoughts. He counted the country's top poets, artists, historians, scholars, and political theorists as his close personal friends.

He was the first Ansary and one of the first Afghans of nonroyal blood to study in the West, where he got two degrees, both I think from Tufts University in Medford,

Massachusetts: a Ph.D. in political science and a dentist's license. When he came back to Kabul, he set up as the country's first dental clinic, but he found that the aristocrats who sought his services would not schedule appointments. They expected to arrive and be examined at once, no matter who was there before them; perhaps, in fact, they relished being served out of order, because what's the use of power if you can't inconvenience someone with it? Khan Kaka could not refuse to see aristocrats, so he expressed his displeasure in a less direct manner. He closed his office and refused to practice dentistry ever again.

Throughout his life, he attended conferences in the West, one or two a year. I have the vague impression they were conferences about Third World development, global food policies, UNESCO projects, and the like. His expenses were paid; he saved what he could from his per diems, and those dollars, converted to Afghan currency, amounted to a handsome sum and provided the bulk of his living.

He owned vineyards in our ancestral village, but those were managed by a poor relation, who kept most of the profits for himself. My uncle knew but looked the other way. "The poor man needs it more than I do," he said.

Another of Khan Kaka's acts of charity was hateful to us children. There was a barber around town by the name of Chighil. This fellow had some disability that made his hands tremble. Nobody wanted a barber with trembling and at times spastic hands working scissors around their head. So my uncle hired him, because otherwise, how would a guy like that make a living? And all the rest of the family fell in line, so Chighil became the Ansary family barber, and woe was us on days when Chighil came around. We had to march to our haircuts, from which we would emerge with badly chopped hair and bleeding skulls.

In later years, Khan Kaka served for a time as an adviser to the Ministry of Education. Someone in the government talked him into it. He went to work for thirty days, but on the thirty-first, he sent word that he was sick. His sickness lasted a month. Finally, a government official came to the compound to ask Khan Kaka if he was ever going to return to work. He said, no, he didn't think he'd ever feel up to it. The official asked if he would be willing to perform his advisory duties from the compound. So Khan Kaka became a vague consultant type for most of the rest of his life.

Khan Kaka's compound, built earlier than ours, followed the traditional design. It had two buildings and two courtyards. The front building ran like a wall across the entire yard, keeping the inner courtyard perfectly private. Outsiders could safely enter the front door and reach the public room reserved for visitors without ever glimpsing the women's world. At the very back of the inner courtyard were two rooms on either side of a short hall. On one side lived Khan Kaka, lord of the household. On the other side lived my grandmother, the soul of the household.

We knew my grandmother as K'koh, but this was only her *luqub,* her family nickname. I don't know her real name and she herself may have forgotten it. To me, she always looked about two hundred years old, but I guess she was only in her fifties in my first years. My grandfather acquired her when she was about five and *he* was in his fifties. Let me explain what I mean by "acquired."

My grandfather was a physician attached to the court—what the West would call a "healer" rather than a doctor. He knew a lot about herbs, "Greek medicine" (as Afghans called the medical lore of Indian civilization—perhaps to avoid calling it Hindu medicine), and the theories of medieval Arabic thinkers. He was also well versed in the charms and spells of Islamic folklore; he knew how to soothe bee stings and cure snakebites.

He was close friends with the royal tax collector. One year the king, a formidable giant named Abdur Rahman, went to war against the Hazaras, a pocket of Mongolian people in central Afghanistan. The king's forces were victorious. The Hazara lords were removed from power and their lands given to royal relatives and their retainers. For some time afterward, when these new aristocrats wanted servants, they'd dip into Hazara families and take as many children as they needed; they would give one another Hazara children as tokens of respect, much as one might send flowers after a social occasion in America, by way of saying thank you.

With the Hazaras subdued, the king wanted to assess how much could be squeezed out of them in revenues, so he sent his tax collector on a tour of the region. My grandfather went along. At some point, they were staying at the home of a village chieftain, who fell ill. My grandfather exercised his healing wisdom, and the chieftain recovered, whereupon he gave my grandfather a little Hazara girl.

My grandfather took the girl with him when he returned to Kabul. They were traveling on horses, of course, with pack donkeys carrying their goods and supplies, and I imagine that she made the journey on one of those donkeys, perhaps nestled in a saddlebag, with thirty pounds of wheat on the other side to counterbalance her.

He stopped at his own village near Kabul. Being a big shot at court, my grandfather didn't spend much time in the village himself. He lived in Kabul mostly. But he had three wives and a compound for each of them in the village, for he was a good Muslim; and Islam orders that a man may not marry more than one wife unless he can treat them all equally. My grandfather discharged this religious duty by setting up a separate household for each of his wives to rule. He dropped off the little Hazara girl at one of these compounds.

Six or seven years later, she was a nubile adolescent. She'd spent all those years toiling like Cinderella at the bottom of the social ladder in a household where her needs must have come last. And then one day, my grandfather came to that compound and asked to see the girl.

She was frightened. She didn't want to look attractive to the Great Man. She didn't know what could lie at the end of that road for her. When the Great Man's summons filtered down to her through attentive layers of family and poor relations, she went to the fire pit and smeared her face with ashes so that she would not look beautiful.

But when she arrived in his presence, she radiated right through the ashes. He saw through the coal dust, the dishevelment of hair, and the humble clothes, and his heart, or perhaps his lust, chose her. He married her within the year. I have often wondered how and why a man in his position would take up with a slave he had acquired in payment for good doctoring. Considering that she was a servant in his household, I have to believe his marrying her must have caused a frightful scandal, but on this, the family chronicles are silent. I want to believe that something happened to him, that he couldn't resist going all the way with her. No, not all the way to sex—that's not so very far to go. I'm talking about further: all the way to the full embrace, the "You be mine" and "I be yours." I want to believe that between those two, love broke out.

My grandfather was probably in his sixties by then, but he sired five sons with K'koh. When he died, the other three wives turned on her. Their sons broke open the little trunk where she kept her only possessions—a few items of jewelry, her spare dress, perhaps a set of prayer beads—looking for the gold and gems they believed my grandfather had given her, or at least for the potions she must have used to bewitch him so. The harassment got so bad, she had to leave the village and move to Kabul, a widowed mother of five. There my grandfather's buddy the royal tax collector took her on as a servant. From that thin ledge on the cliff of a widow's life in Afghanistan, she deployed her sons. One went into the army, one into government service, and three to school and then abroad.

Ten years later, her first son was a general, her second the celebrated intellectual Khan Kaka, her third a successful government official, her fourth the dean of the College of Literature at Kabul University, and her youngest a mathematics student in Switzerland.

The other wives? Still living in the village, along with their sons.

My eldest uncle, the general, was exactly the opposite of our little Napoléon. Jan Agha—"Dear Father"—was impossibly handsome even in his last days: large, grim, muscular, physical, and tough. Unlike Khan Kaka the confirmed bachelor, Jan Agha married twice and had twelve children, three by his first wife and, after she died, nine more by her niece, whom he married next.

In his youth, Jan Agha performed an act of legendary bravery. He was a student at the military college on the outskirts of Kabul in 1929 when the rural bandit known as the Water-Carrier's Son raised an army against the monarchy and swept across the countryside. The foppish King Amanullah, Abdur Rahman's grandson, escaped to Italy. The rebel army began to move on Kabul. Most of the students and all of the teachers in the military academy fled. Only my uncle and two other boys stayed behind and defended the school: three teenagers against a horde. They stockpiled guns and ammunition at various windows and ran from one to another, firing shots, hoping to fool the Water-Carrier's Son into thinking they were a regiment. They halted the army for a couple of days, but eventually they fell asleep and were captured. The Water-Carrier's Son did not punish the boys, however. He praised them for their loyalty. "You have eaten the king's salt," he said. "You were honor-bound to fight for him to the end."

My uncle stayed in the military, and after the monarchy was restored, he rose in the ranks until he became a general. Even then, however, he was overmatched by his second wife, Mahgul. Talk about formidable. Mahgul was Elizabeth Taylor–beautiful (and remains striking even today, in her mid-seventies). She bore my uncle nine children, and after he died, she astounded the family by declaring that she was going to go to school now. She started first grade in her late thirties, learned to read, and got a government job. When the Russians invaded Afghanistan, she escaped to the West with the help of her many children, settled in Portland, Oregon (but later moved to Washington, D.C.), and secured American citizenship, even though she could barely speak English, scoring better on her citizenship test than her educated children, nephews, and nieces—as she never tired of telling us.

Imposing as she was, Mahgul was not the only matriarch in our clan. Koko Gul, for example, was another redoubtable one: Deep, crafty, and acerbically witty, this woman would have cut a great groove in the world as a general, a politician, an artist, or who knows what, if only she had been a man. But because she was a woman, her canvas was the inner life of the family village, and it was in the clan that she created her masterpieces—intricate deals, matches, marriages, and alliances, joining one part of the clan to another. She was a weaver, you might say, and our clan was her tapestry.

She had been married to one of the Ansary half brothers, but she judged him a village bumpkin; she wanted a man who was going places. She went to the village judge and accused her husband of impotence, one of the grounds on which a woman could sue for divorce under Islamic law. There was nothing the poor man could do to disprove the accusation, so she got her freedom, and a short time later, she married my uncle Shaghah.

I could go on like this for hours. But my elders in those old days could have gone on for days. Endlessly, we told and retold our family stories, honing them into folklore, absorbing them into the soil from which grew our greater self, the tree of which we were just the buds, the leaves, the branches.

GERM OF THE WEST

I WAS BORN into that world when it was virtually untouched by the West. I emphasize the word *virtually.* Some penetration had already occurred—my sister and I embodied it. Not only was our mother American; she was the only American woman in Kabul when she arrived there in 1945.

Because of my mother, my sister and I gravitated to the few English speakers we could find. My first best friend was a boy named Jeff. His mother was British, and it goes without saying that the only two women in Kabul who spoke English forged a friendship, even if their accents didn't match. I can't picture Jeff, and I remember nothing about him except that we raced toy cars down the rows of "elephant foot" patterns on the Afghan carpet in our living room.

But even though I can't picture him, I *almost* remember

him. And in that state of almost remembering, I capture flickers of strange, deep, dreamlike emotions and of prehistoric imagery—the afternoon light on the varnished arms of the couch in our living room, the meaningless tinkle of our mothers' voices somewhere outside the bubble of our Neverland . . . a primal memory of fun.

When I was seven years old, another American family, the Fritzes, came to Kabul. Dale Fritz was an eccentric inventor, a junkyard tinkerer. Twentieth-century America had no honored place for such a man, so Dale surveyed the world for a nation that might need him, and Afghanistan caught his notice.

He had come to Kabul to invent things Afghan peasants could make with the materials and know-how they already possessed. He made no effort to sell his inventions, as he didn't care about money. What he liked to do was take one of his devices—a pump, say—down to any old bazaar, put it together in the main thoroughfare, and use it, so that the gawking crowd could see what it did. Then he'd break it down and give it away. He couldn't explain how the pump worked, because he didn't speak any of the languages of Afghanistan. He hoped to disseminate his inventions through folk culture.

And it worked. Years later, my father had occasion to drive Land Rovers to villages so remote that when he arrived, the people asked after the health of Amanullah, that king who had been deposed thirty years earlier. Yet these villagers were using, and indeed making, the Dale Fritz pump!

Dale Fritz and his buoyant country-Christian wife,

Merle, had a boy, Roger, and a girl, Karen. In our family, we had a boy, Tamim, and a girl, Rebecca. The Fritz children were eight and six. Rebecca and I were nine and seven, respectively. No wonder we all formed a deathless friendship.

My Afghan friends included mainly my baker's dozen of cousins (their number eventually increased to about twenty-five). Three of my male cousins, Najib, Mazar, and Aziz, were almost exactly my age, and we formed a little gang of four, roaming the compounds together during the big weddings, stealing grapes and mulberries from our neighbors' walled gardens during outings to Deh Yahya, our ancestral village.

When the cousins weren't around, my most immediate buddy in those earliest years was Suleiman Shah, a boy who lived in our compound, the son of our *kinar-nisheen*. He and I started school the same year, so every morning we walked the mile or two from our compound to Chamchamast Elementary together. On the way, we played a game that consisted of tossing empty glass bottles onto the path ahead and then trying to hit and break the other's bottle. We crossed only one bit of pavement on the way to school. All the rest of the way, we ambled along on a dirt path that snaked between compound walls, through somnolent bazaars, and across little gullies, streams, and irrigation ditches. Generations of bare feet had worn this trail into a shallow trough that brimmed with fine silty dust in the summer. Every time our bottles landed, they raised powdery clouds.

Once we got to school, another walled compound with a dusty yard and a few willow trees, we boys all lined up in two long rows outdoors, and the head teacher inspected our fingernails. If he found any dirt, he barked, "Palm!" The guilty boy then had to present his outstretched palm, and the teacher whacked it with a whiplike stick cut from one of the willow trees, which were grown in the school yard for this sole purpose.

After inspection, we repaired to the bare classrooms of unpainted adobe with uneven brick floors. We sat in rows, two boys to a desk. At school, I always felt gawky and out of place, because my mother dressed me in American clothes, which set me apart, and my hair was still rather blond. And besides, all the boys knew I was the *kharijai*, the foreign one, and they gave me a jocular hard time about it.

We had only one book each: our reader. The rest of our schoolwork consisted of oral recitation in Farsi. In math class, the teacher would write a times table on the board and then read it aloud, and we would repeat his words in a chorus. In Koran class, we repeated each of the first ten verses in Arabic until we had learned them by heart. There was also a separate class in *qui'raut*, or Koranic recitation, a melodic and highly dramatic way of chanting the Koran. None of us spoke Arabic, so we didn't know what those melodic syllables meant, but those students who were good at *qui'raut* could stir thrilling emotions in the rest of us purely with the sounds they made. I was conspicuously incompetent at this.

Next came religion class, in which we learned the duties of a Muslim. All our other teachers wore European mufti, but the stern black-bearded religion teacher came to us clad in the traditional Afghan outfit: long shirt, baggy pants, and turban. Sometimes, if we were lucky, he would tell us gripping stories about the Prophet and the early days of Islam. These stories only added to impressions we brought from home, since religious stories, no less than family stories, were part of the lore of the compounds.

Indeed, Prophet Muhammad felt like one of the figures in my personal life, someone I knew, a really great guy, but just a regular guy: warm and loving, irritable sometimes when he had too much on his mind, hassled by family life, yes, and yet so touchingly dependent on his wife Khadija (originally his employer), a loving father apt to tease the kids—very human, in short. The revelations he delivered came straight from God, but he was never tempted to claim any divinity for himself. How many people would have possessed such restraint?

After his death, Muhammad was succeeded by a series of four spiritual leaders, or *khalifahs* (caliphs), and from my milieu, I formed distinct impressions of them, too. First came Muhammad's father-in-law Abu Bakr, who was an old man when he took over, and I thought of him as a wise elder. Respect—that's the emotion I felt for Abu Bakr. Vis-à-vis Muhammad, he was a father figure.

Abu Bakr died two years after Muhammad. Then Omar took over—dashing, irresistible Omar, my favorite *khalifah*. I don't know if the scholars agree with me, but I always thought of him as Muhammad's best friend. He was, however, best friend raised to mythological stature. A great general, he led Arab armies deep into Egypt and Iran, yet I never thought of him as coercive. His authority rested purely on greatness of soul, combined with the kind of gentleness that comes from confident inner strength.

The legend of Khalifah Omar supports the Muslim belief that the sudden emergence of the Islamic "empire" represents not a military conquest but a vast spiritual awakening. Islam arose in the seventh century among a relatively small group of poor people—a few tens of thousands, at most—who squeezed out a living between two wealthy powers, the Sassanids of Persia and the Byzantines of Asia Minor. Yet within two generations, the Arabs had vanquished both powers and presided over a realm, and with it a coherent culture, that stretched from Turkey to Spain. It was as if, at the height of the Cold War, Fiji had come up with a colorful new ideology and toppled both the United States and the Soviet Union.

How did it happen? Most Muslims believe that the Arab armies prevailed because they brought a vision of social order so appealing that the native people overthrew their rulers so as to embrace Islam. Outsiders might consider this a religious fantasy, but it does help explain an apparent miracle.

I remember an anecdote I heard about early Islam. A

pompous agent of an exalted monarch of a pompous and exalted state went to Medina to negotiate with Khalifah Omar. He reined up his horse next to a bunch of guys who were sitting in the shade along a wall, trading tales and cracking jokes like small-town geezers in a lemonade commercial. "Get up," he ordered. "Take me to Omar Ibn Al Khatib, leader of the Muslim community, supreme commander of the empire that stretches from Anatolia to Africa." One of the old geezers stood up, dusted off his trousers, and said, "I'm Omar. What do you want?"

It pleases me still to imagine the social spirit that might enable the leader of a vast and powerful political community to loll about, between state duties, with a random group of citizens, cracking jokes and trading gossip, not only indistinguishable from them to an outsider but treated as nothing special or fearful by them. It also pleases me to think that in the early Islamic empire, what really conquered the Sassanids and the Byzantines was this social spirit. And for me, Omar as a personality stands for that face of Islam: earthy, pleasant, unpretentious, generous, fair, friendly, exuberant . . . and brilliant, as well.

Omar was succeeded by Uthman, whom I always considered a dark figure among the first four *khalifahs*. Uthman had scholars consolidate and record the revelations, which became the first standard Koran. He also set others to compiling and authenticating Muhammad's sayings and customs. You might call him the Saint Paul figure of early Islam. From the point of Islam as dogma, I suppose Uthman played a crucial role. But I never liked him much personally, and neither did someone else, because Uthman was assassinated.

Then came Ali, the fourth *khalifah,* and with him came the great rift in the Muslim world. The rift actually began when Muhammad died. One faction had taken the Prophet at his word when he said he was just a regular guy. They believed his power lay entirely in his message. Another faction said nah, a mystical force must have been incarnated in him and that light must now be incarnate in someone else. The community, they said, could not *elect* a leader. God had already appointed one, just as God had chosen Muhammad. The community had only the duty to *recognize* him. This faction felt the new leader had to be Muhammad's son-in-law Ali.

So they felt grumbly when the bulk of the community handed the mantle to Abu Bakr, but they bit their tongues and bided their time, because Abu Bakr was old. He wouldn't last. When Abu Bakr died, the mantle passed to Omar, which galled Ali's partisans, but again they bit their tongues, because who could gainsay the greatness of Omar? But when Omar died and the nod went to Uthman, it was too much. Uthman was a leading member of Quraysh, the aristocratic tribe of Mecca, the people who had tried to assassinate the Prophet.

To the partisans, or *shi'ah,* of Ali, Uthman's election represented the reassertion of the status quo. The Quraysh had joined the ranks of Islam, and now they were taking over again. You can see why this would chafe.

Frankly, I always saw a youth-versus-age dichotomy

here. Ali represented, to my mind, that teenage impulse of spiritual-revolution-forever. Uthman, by contrast, was the emissary of the levelheaded adults, who always want to clean up the detritus of the party, take stock, put things away, and vacuum the living room in case guests arrive. Looking back, I think he stood for that ever-powerful urge in human affairs: back to normal.

All of human history can be seen, can it not, as an argument between those who try to explode the existing forms and those who try to freeze things as they are. The second impulse always wins in the end, except it's never the end. The cosmic winner is always change, except change can never settle in as the permanent state. History is a river, except people can live only in lakes, so they dam the current and build villages by still waters—but the dam always breaks. And always, some folks ride the flood, screaming slogans and exulting. Ultimately, those folk disappear in the foam and tumult, and when the waves die down, you always find the bureaucrats in charge again, saying, "Okay, we've slipped downstream, but this is where we should build our Permanent Home."

Permanent Home, the impossible dream.

When Uthman was murdered, Ali finally got his turn. Poor Ali. If Abu Bakr was the father figure, Omar the best friend, and Uthman the somber stepuncle, Ali was the archetypal son. I picture him as dark and passionate, with melancholy, romantic eyes, radiating warmth and masculinity, loving, earnest, and deep. To me, he's always been the man who feels too much, cares too much, and calculates too little. He plunges into life, opening his heart to strangers, and lets the chips fall where they may.

Ali never really established himself. Uthman had appointed his relatives to high positions throughout the growing Muslim empire, and one of these relatives, the governor of Syria, disputed Ali's claim to the caliphate. He met Ali on the field of battle with an impressive army, and Ali agreed to negotiate, which disillusioned his closest followers—God's representative on Earth, compromising with some sword-swinging jerk? No way! Renegades from his own *shi'ah* sect assassinated him, and Islam's spiritual golden age came to an end. But ever since, Islam has been divided into the Shiite Muslims, who backed Ali, and the Sunni Muslims, who backed the first three *khalifahs*. My family were Sunnis, as are most Afghans.

All this was just some of the history we learned at our religion class in the school in Kabul. Sometimes the religion teacher also told us stories that illustrated doctrinal points. The one I remember best still makes me sweat.

First some context. As a child, I was a miser, saving money relentlessly in hopes of someday buying something grand. And the grand thing I craved at this time was a box of watercolor paints, the kind with little round cakes of color arranged in two rows and a brush that lies in its own little gutter between them. A year of scrimping and hoarding had brought me within five afghanis—about a dime—of this prize. Well, one day, in my parents' bedroom, I saw a bundle of cash on their chest of drawers, including a five-afghani bill, which I pocketed. I waited to get caught, but no one said anything. One day, some grown-up took me to the shops in Shar-i-Nau, and there I bought the paints. No one asked how a seven-year-old who had saved only ninety cents in a year could have saved another dime in a week. No one even seemed to be tracking how much money I had. I took the paints home, feeling breathless. It looked like I was going to get away with it!

The next day, I must have had a premonition. I said my stomach hurt, but I had no fever, so I had to go to school. I passed fingernail inspection, but the boy next to me got a beating and I felt guilty. Why?

The day passed in somnolent boredom until religion class. Then the black-bearded teacher put away his manuals and postponed a test on the prayer ritual in order to tell us a story. Ordinarily, this would have been a relief, because, as the obvious foreigner in the class, I was always singled out for the sternest testing. But this time, I felt uneasy.

He told us about a kid who stole some money from his parents, a good kid, basically, but a kid who wanted some trifling trinket. In a moment of weakness—because the cash was just sitting there unattended, because nobody would ever know—he slipped the money into his pocket, went to the bazaar, and bought his bauble. But soon he wanted something else, as lust-crazed moral weaklings will. And so he needed to steal again. The first time, he'd had to go through some mental acrobatics to convince himself that stealing from his parents would be okay, but now his soul was inured to arguments of conscience. He sneaked into his parents' room without qualms, stole the money, and went out to satisfy his brutish cravings.

So he slipped from bad to worse, until a day came when he wanted something, and only one way lay open to satisfy his corrupt desires. The teacher described this next part in lingering detail—how the boy sharpened the knife; how he parted the curtains to look in on his moonlit sleeping parents, how even then a stirring to righteousness trembled in his soul, only to be buried by his animal desires grown monstrous; how he tiptoed into the room. The moonlight glinted on the knife. He brought it down, into his father's throat, into his mother's, into his father's again—

The religion teacher stopped, stroked his beard, and glared—directly at me. "Learn a lesson from this story, boys. Never give in to any temptation whatsoever. If you steal five afghanis today, you will end up murdering your own dear parents someday—because the path to evil is steep, and once you set foot upon it, you cannot easily climb back."

I was so sick by the time I got home, I threw up. I went to bed, and in the morning claimed I couldn't get up. Again, I had no fever, but my mother found my agonized writhings convincing and agreed to let me stay home. She offered to stay with me, but I wanted her gone. I really didn't want to kill her, and according to my religion teacher, even though I felt no urge to kill her now, if it came down to me, her, and a sharp knife alone in the same room, all bets were off.

It sounds comical today, but at age seven, I wasn't laughing, and forty-six years have not dimmed the message.

MORTALITY

ONE DAY IN 1957, when I was in third grade, my father's best friend, Abdul Kayeum, came to see him. Kayeum and my father had gone to America together, and now the government had given Kayeum the most prestigious job in Afghanistan. They had tapped him to run the Helmand Valley Authority, and he wanted my father to come aboard as his deputy.

The Helmand Valley Authority was a development project funded by the United States. It proposed to duplicate California's Imperial Valley "miracle" in Afghanistan by using the waters of the Helmand River to irrigate the country's only flat region, a hellishly hot stony desert near the border with Iran. About this land, certain stories were told, stories that went back a thousand years, to the days of the Ghaznavid Empire. In San Francisco not long ago, I saw a high school world history textbook that covered the

Ghaznavid Empire with a single picture and a short caption, but in central Asia, it was a mighty big deal for a hundred years. It stretched from India to the Caspian Sea, covering an area perhaps half the size of the United States. Its kings, or sultans, loomed large as patrons of the arts. Sultan Mahmud had nine hundred poets living at his court, plus innumerable historians, philosophers, and the like. *The Book of Kings,* the major epic of Persian literature, was originally written for him.

The Ghaznavids and their successors, the Seljuk Turks, presided over three hundred years of art and thought every bit as vital as the Italian Renaissance. The Renaissance, however, segued into "the European expansion," which became the main stem of world history. The first Islamic civilization of the Turks, Arabs, and Persians was cut short and buried by the Mongol holocaust.

At this remove, Genghis Khan registers as romantic to many. "Great conqueror. Great strategist," the textbooks say, forgetting to add, "Mindless destroyer. Brutal butcher." Genghis Khan destroyed so utterly, on such a scale, that no one today can know what Islamic civilization was about or where it was going then. Imagine if a massive force of slobbering boors had invaded Europe during the Renaissance and erased from *memory* Leonardo da Vinci, Michelangelo, Raphael, Botticelli, Dante, Shakespeare, Chaucer, Erasmus, Venice, Genoa, Florence, and Rome. That's pretty much what the Mongols did to Islamic civilization. In Afghanistan alone, the Mongols dumped the once-celebrated library of the now-forgotten city of Balkh into the Amu, a river so broad, you can't see from one bank to the other, and yet the library of ancient Balkh dammed its waters for three days (and then washed away).

The Ghaznavids established a regional capital in that hellish desert, where they built enormous irrigation works that used the Helmand River to create, according to legend, "the breadbasket of Asia." But Genghis Khan didn't like bread. He thought people should herd sheep and eat meat. So he tore up the irrigation systems, killed every living thing in the local cities, right down to the dogs and cats, and then sowed salt in the soil. The region never recovered.

In the 1950s, however, inspired by the legend of those ancient irrigation works, the Afghan government conceived a fantasy of restoring the breadbasket. They would sell the harvest for cash abroad, use the currency to buy machines, and transform Afghanistan into a country as modern as Turkey. This was the vision that enraptured the royal family of Afghanistan, and out of the ranks of the Western-educated commoners, they plucked my father's friend Dr. Abdul Kayeum to serve as president of the project. They put him in charge of making it all happen, and Kayeum came to my father; and so our family got caught in the swirl of a royal dream, which elevated my father to the vice presidency of the Helmand Valley Authority.

My sister and I vaguely understood that my father's promotion raised our status in Afghanistan, and we were glad. We would be moving to the tiny town of Lashkargah, where half the people would be Americans, and we looked

forward to that prospect. We worried, however, about losing the two precious Americans we already had—our dear-
est friends, Roger and Karen Fritz.

Every day, we and the Fritzes played together, in our
compound or in theirs, walking atop the walls, lolling
in our tree houses, catching frogs in the big irrigation
well. When the adults made us separate each day, we
felt wrenching loss, because tomorrow was always so far
away, and it was easy to believe we'd never see them
again, and if we didn't, breath itself would be cut in half,
sunlight would dim, food lose its taste, and aromas vanish.
We were pretty sure we were never going to die, or at least
that we'd live to a hundred, which was practically the same
thing, but we worried about this other form of mortality—
saying good-bye. We'd tasted mild doses of it already, and
now we were facing *good-bye forever.*

Forever had a particular resonance for Rebecca and me
as Afghans. Islamic lore and the Sufi heritage of our family
in particular—Sufism being a tradition of mysticism and
poetry in Islam—told us that life was a dream whose only
true trait was *migzarad:* "flows on past." The real lay elsewhere.

The melancholy of *migzarad* suffused our feelings
about losing the Fritzes, and also about having to abandon
our dear Afghan hound—which was not freakishly elon-
gated, longhaired, groomed to perfection, and dressed in a
satin warm-up jacket like the Afghan hounds you see in
America. Afghanistan had no tradition of dog shows or
show dogs, and *tazis* served as hunting dogs to aristocrats,

so they were bred for strength, speed, and smarts, not bizarreness.

We had acquired the dog a year or two earlier. When my proud father first brought the dog home, he wanted to demonstrate its acrobatic skills, so he flung up a chunk of bread, and the dog snatched it out of the air. Then we flung up hunks of bread, and the dog leaped high and snatched them out of the air, too, wolfing them down before its paws touched again upon the green-and-white tiles of our veranda in that fading afternoon.

"Let's call him Hungry," someone suggested, and so we did—until we discovered that "he" was a she, at which point her name became Hungria. She lived in the yard, of course, for dogs were never allowed indoors in Afghanistan, any more than horses are seated at the breakfast table in America. But Rebecca and I practically moved out to the yard to live with her. We snuggled against the warmth of her big body in her dust bowl bed, and we made up for our deficiency in toys by incorporating her puppies into our games.

Lashkargah was a three-day journey across uncertain terrain, and it would be hard enough to move our furniture all that way, much less a dog. Hungria would have to stay behind. But we did not protest or misbehave. As Afghan children, Rebecca and I did not expect our wishes to count. We just shared the towering profundity of our loss, tasting that resignation to fate that came to us from our Afghan soil, for even as children, we knew that loss would deepen us. That's what it means to be an Afghan.

On the scales of life, sorrow is all in one pan—the world; God always outweighs the world, and with ease. Submission to loss brings one closer to the real.

This belief system did, I think, provide good tools for dealing with sadness. But my sister and I were operating out of two tool kits. Our Afghan side would say, "Ah, the loss!" but where a fully Afghan response would have added, "I surrender to *you*, Allah," our American side, as derived from our skeptical mother, cut in with "And then you die. The end."

I once asked Mommy about these remarkable stories I'd been hearing, stories of an enormous fellow who watched us from the sky day and night, reaching down sometimes through the blue ceiling, his fingers so huge and yet so delicate, they could grab one small boy by his bangs—or, if Suleiman Shah was to be believed, simply scooped one up with a big ladle. Could this be true?

"Well," said my mother evasively, "some people believe X, and some people believe Y." In short, I got a lecture on comparative religion. But I didn't care who believed what; I wanted to know what was *true*. Mommy was the only authority I could trust on such a fundamental matter, and her answer conveyed to me the coded message: "Above you, only sky."

Daddy took Hungria away three days before we left for Lashkargah. She came bounding to his whistle, he opened the car door for her, and she scrambled in trustingly. Then he and the driver took off with our dog.

Hours later, my father came back with the chauffeur

but no dog. Over dinner, he told us he had given Hungria to a man who lived in a village some fifty miles from the city. Fifty miles, in that world of donkey tracks and dirt roads, was a lot of miles.

Our remaining days in Kabul inched past, and Hungria's absence throbbed like a toothache. My Afghan philosophic melancholy bore down on me, a world of weight that God never showed up to outweigh. Nothing tempered the grief except my brother Riaz, who was almost one year old now, and whom Rebecca and I loved even more than we had ever cared for Hungria's puppies.

The night before we were to leave, we were in the yard with the Fritz children, playing out the trembling intensity of the Last Good-bye. In this drama, our friendship had cosmic significance: Never again would the universe duplicate the pregnant encounter of four such mated souls, and now we were to be torn asunder by shadowy forces so enormous, they dwarfed even our titanic adults. We felt like outsize heroes and yet, at the same time, like insignificant specks, ground to dust beneath the wheels of inexorable kismet.

Dusk descended, but we played on in the inky darkness enclosed between the far-flung walls of our Ansary compound. Beyond the walls, a profound silence thickened the air, for this was Kabul—a big city, yes, but a city virtually without cars or machinery, without electricity or factories. What noise could there have been at this time of night? Only the distant hubbub of people speaking and moving, and even that had subsided in a city lit by oil lamps.

And then, in this silence, we heard—even from the
meadow south of our house, maybe six hundred feet distant from our compound door—a testament to the silence
of a Kabul night: a sound of dog nails scratching on wood.

We rushed to that enormous door of solid heartwood
to find out who was calling, scratching. It was Hungria, of
course. Oh my God, what did this do to the melancholy of
our Afghan temperament? She was wet, and cold, and hungry and inarticulate. She could not tell us what rivers she
had crossed or what mountains she had climbed. Hungria
could only tell us by her mute, shivering presence that she
was not going to submit to loss. I drew a pivotal lesson that
night when Hungria bounded in upon me: that in this
streaming dream we call the world, there is some rock after
all. We had tried to give Hungria away, but she wouldn't
stay away. We had tried to get rid of her, but she had for-
given that unforgivable act. She had conquered mountains
and rivers and even the darkness of our duplicitous hearts
to find us again. Love, she said, has power against sorrow. I
believe that Hungria handed me a challenge that night:
You say you're faithful? Clear this bar. A dog did it. Can
you?

AMERICAN LASHKARGAH

OUR THREE-DAY JOURNEY from Kabul to Lash-kargah took us across the very desert the Helmand Valley Authority was supposed to transform. Rebecca and I nestled in the back seat, telling stories, playing games, and making up jokes. I remember how hysterically funny it was to pretend each other's chins were noses. Sometimes we hugged or tickled Riaz, who was back there with us. My father drove with one hand on the wheel, his face pensive and bemused. My mother, hair bound in a kerchief, glowed with good humor, for we were going to a town where she could be with Americans again.

We cruised over flat soil littered with embedded stones and baked as hard as potter's clay by a sun that routinely drove summertime temperatures to 110 degrees and more. Nothing poked through the crust except a thigh-high shrub called camel thorn. Once in a while, we saw herds of gazelles bounding weightlessly across the landscape. Sometimes the noise of the engine scared up a flock of big-winged birds or sent flurries of dust-colored quail skittering through the underbrush. There was nothing else to see except the shimmering mirage that flowed across the road, always a mile or two ahead.

We moved to Lashkargah around September of 1957. A few years earlier, the government had built this small town from scratch practically overnight. And when I say small, I do mean small. In the United States, a small town has a few blocks of houses, a grocery store, maybe a gas station, a post office, TV and radio stations that connect you to all the wide world, and fifty miles farther on, there is another town, with billboards lining the road between.

Lashkargah was two blocks wide and eight blocks deep—four blocks of stately mansions, where the Americans and the Afghan officials lived, and four blocks of cramped bungalows, which housed the clerks and minor bureaucrats. There was no plane, train, or bus service to Lashkargah. Only one road came in; only one road went out. No telephone or power lines connected us to the outside world.

Lashkargah ended abruptly on every side. One side came to a bluff overlooking the Helmand River, a steep drop to the water. The other three sides were delineated just as sharply by the desert. Walking two blocks north or south from our house literally brought me to the place where the sidewalk ended. From there, I could look across a sea of thorns to the lip of the world.

Just south of town was a pitiful bazaar, thirty or forty stalls flanking a dirt path that straggled along the river. From the last of these, you could just make out the ruins of the ancient city that still hulked along the riverbank for miles, the winter capital of the Ghaznavids, deserted nine hundred years ago, now home only to jackals and wild boar.

We bought our meat and bread and vegetables from that small bazaar, but I never wondered where the shopkeepers went at night—they certainly never came into the American part of Lashkargah, where we lived; they weren't allowed there. Much later, I learned that a few miles north, just over the horizon, next to the river, there was a traditional Afghan village like our own Deh Yahya. Some of the villagers came to Lashkargah to work as gardeners or servants, but they had to go straight to their employers' houses and then right out again; they couldn't linger in Lashkargah or roam our streets. To the HVA, that traditional village didn't exist.

Our house in Lashkargah dwarfed the one in our compound in Kabul, a testament to our new importance. It had thirteen rooms and a back yard that ran to the escarpment bordering the river. From our porch, I could see a thrilling sight—the neighbor's house, and the street, too, and anyone walking on it. And the neighbors could see us; no one in Lashkargah had walls around their yard except the Kayeums, and their walls were low, almost ceremonial.

Because we had such a big house, it was no longer necessary for my sister and me to share a bedroom, which was like saying "no longer necessary to play or sing." In fact, I was now sharing my bedroom with Riaz, who was just a baby; he didn't count as human company. And then I had another tiny room that was mine alone—my laboratory, the family called it. Rebecca and I were so close, however, that away from her, I felt like a body separated from its heart. But I soon discovered that an air shaft connected our two rooms. Late at night, when the world was asleep, we'd whisper together through this shaft: news, gossip, feelings. Our voices carried perfectly.

Strangely enough, none of the Afghan officials in Lashkargah except my father and Dr. Kayeum had school-age children—and they both had American wives. So we and the Kayeum children were now positioned to join the tiny American community.

The day we arrived, Rona and Marya Kayeum took Rebecca and me to meet the American kids. Oh, how I anticipated that moment! All my life, Rebecca and I had been the strange ones who wore the funny clothes, ate with forks, always went home with their mommy and daddy at night, because we were the American ones. Now, at last, we were on our way to join not just a friend or two like Jeff or the Fritzes but a whole *community* of people like us. The Kayeums must have known how we felt, since they too were Afghan-Americans, but on that walk, they stayed curiously silent.

We found the Americans two blocks east of the river— about ten of them, boys and girls, ducking in and out of a "clubhouse" that melted my heart with envy. I had always dreamed of having just such a place. It was an authentic kid-sized house, with a roof and windows. The walls were only three feet high, but the floor was sunken about three feet deep, as I could see through the leprechaun's door that stood ajar at the bottom of steps carved into the dirt. It looked to be quite spacious inside. Right away, two hefty girls with dirty-blond hair, big arms, and potato noses told us that the American boys and girls went down into that clubhouse to have sex, whatever that meant. It sounded intriguingly American. I wanted to go down there and have some of that sex, too.

But suddenly, a freckle-faced boy stuck his head out the door and roared ferociously, "Don't let those dirty Afghans in here!" I was shocked and confused—not just that he was calling Afghans dirty but that he was calling us Afghans. After all, among the Afghans, we were Americans; so if we weren't Americans, either, what were we?

Despite the rough welcome, our world became the American part of Lashkargah. We virtually never stepped across the line into that humbler half of town. Over the months and years, we wormed our way in with the American kids, and our status among them rose, by seniority, as it were. You see, the American families came to Lashkargah on staggered two-year contracts, so every few months one of them was leaving and a new one arriving. And when new American kids arrived, we and the Kayeum kids were always there to greet them, show them the ropes. We evolved into the old-timers.

Yet we remained Americans with an asterisk. Unmistakable differences marked us off. The Americans, for example, could shop in the PX and we couldn't. They had canned foods, and blue jeans, and Coca-Cola; we didn't.

The American moms ran a home school in one of the houses, and we went there for a few months while a new school for Afghans was being built. The schoolhouse was just one of the residential buildings, with all the rooms converted to classroom use. It had maps, globes, and new textbooks, not to mention paper, notebooks, art supplies, and reference books. The rooms smelled of chalk, linoleum, and Formica. We sang songs and had midmorning milk breaks and graham cracker snacks. But I guess it didn't look right for the children of the two top Afghan officials to study with foreigners, so we were pulled out, and after that we studied at home, using hand-me-down materials from the Americans. At home, my mother and Joan Kayeum taught us an American curriculum: history, geography, math, grammar, and the like—no more Islamic history, prayers, or theology. Tutors came in to teach us Pashto, the local language in this region, and to keep us moving ahead in Farsi literature, but with indifferent success—Farsi as literature dropped out of my sensibilities at this point.

The Afghan school building was finally completed when I was in seventh grade, and I started going there the following year. It was a single solid concrete block poured out in the shape of an H: two quadrangles back to back, some ten minutes east of town. The classrooms had bare, unfinished walls. The windows had no panes. Each room was furnished with thirty or forty chairs, one desk, and a blackboard—nothing else. We had no books. Classes consisted mostly of the teacher dictating chapters from the only textbook in the province, while we students scribbled furiously. Afterward, we compared notes and tried to fill in the gaps.

The HVA's mission, it became apparent, was not just to build dams but to impose Western progress on the Afghan people, and the school was part of the plan. Most of my classmates were not boys, but young men recruited from remote villages in the hinterlands. When I say "recruited," I mean drafted. A jeep full of soldiers would screech into a village. A government rep would hop out and order the village headman to line up the young men. When they had assembled, he would ask them a few questions and make his choices on the spot: "You, you, and you—get your stuff. You're going to school."

Then the jeep would roll on to the next town and the new students would be shipped to Lashkargah, where they were sprayed for lice and issued gray woolen outfits. So it was that most of my eighth-grade classmates were men in their twenties who dressed like Maoist infantry.

They lived like army inductees, too, in a huge dormitory filled to capacity with bunk beds, row upon row. They had virtually nothing to call their own except the beds they slept in. They were free to go anywhere they wanted except into the town of Lashkargah, but there was nowhere else to go except those few blocks of bazaar just south of town.

Sometimes I hung out with my classmates after school.

We played soccer or competed at hurling big stones we gathered from the desert floor. Sometimes we studied together. Only once did I visit their dorm, however. The sight of that big room, those rows of beds, their life, shocked me. Our conversation bristled with discomfort. These fellows were suffering through a hard, strange fate brought upon them by the government and by the HVA, which my father represented.

My father wasn't the top boss, it's true, but he and Kayeum worked as a team. My father quietly managed the project as chief administrator. Kayeum, the politician and dynamic orator, vigorous of body, hawk-nosed and handsome, flamboyantly fronted it.

Once, I remember, my father invited five of the students to our house to honor them quietly for some small achievement—good grades or some such. They were sitting in the living room in their uniforms, sipping tea and nibbling sugar-coated almonds, when Kayeum showed up at the front door on some unrelated business. When he heard about the Afghan students in the next room, he saw a political opportunity and joined them.

The young men felt shy and proud to be socializing with the boss of the HVA, just as army privates might feel if their commander in chief sat down with them. Kayeum asked affably about their families and their health, setting them at ease. He explained to them—his voice gaining a certain fervor—that the Helmand Valley was a dream for Afghanistan dreamed by the king himself. In a few words, he sketched the glorious days of the Ghaznavids, when this valley had been the heart of a vast and civilized empire, and then he sketched a future in which the Helmand Valley would again raise the country up to that cultured grace. Unnoticed in a corner of the room, I listened in, and I, too, felt inspired by the words.

But the king and his dreams were not important, Kayeum went on, and neither was he. The heart of this project was the school, really, and the heartbeat of the school was its students. And out of all the students, Kayeum confided, five stood out. He leaned forward, and so did they. *"Alhamdulillah!"* Kayeum declared—"Praise God!"—for bringing to the school five such talents as these fellows here.

Kayeum had his prayer beads out and was clacking them off with his thumb as he told the students that the fate of the dream lay with them, God permitting. Now his passion drew him to his feet, and they rose, too. He looked them in the eye one by one and swore that he would work tirelessly, by God, to win these boys the future they deserved. He would get them scholarships to study in Europe or America, by God—yes, if he had any power in the matter. They should go from here tonight knowing that they were special, and that while they focused on their studies, somewhere in the world, unseen by them, Kayeum would be laboring on their behalf.

They would have followed him anywhere that night. I had no idea five such luminaries were visiting our house, but in the course of Kayeum's speech, I looked over at them and, yes, I could see the greatness shining in their eyes. Later, however, I overheard Kayeum asking my father who those boys were and what they had done.

Most days, after school, I hung out in those eight blocks of American Lashkargah with American kids my age. We played tennis and lounged around the swimming pool, where only Americans and top Afghan officials were allowed. We rode our bikes. We went to the movies shown on Friday nights at the American staff house. Sometimes the Americans had square dances, and Rebecca and I learned the steps. About once a week, one of the Americans had a party, and every kid in town above the age of ten or so went to it—about twenty kids tops. The parties—"get-togethers," we called them—featured lemonade and homemade ice cream and dancing on someone's veranda in the warm, dry nights to the latest American records. Yes, we had American records, because each time a new American family came to town, they brought the latest hits, so we knew about Elvis Presley and the Everly Brothers, and we could sing along with "Tell Laura I Love Her." Yet I always felt like an American wanna-be, my face pressed to a windowpane, gazing into someone else's living room—I might be just as close to that Coke as someone in the room, but I was separated from it by an invisible sheet.

Then a great thing happened. The year I turned twelve, the Murphy family came to Lashkargah. Dr. Murphy was an authentic do-gooder—that is, his goal in life really was to do good. He came to Lashkargah to open a free medical clinic for Afghans.

The Murphys had five children, including a boy my age. And this boy, Matt, was charisma made manifest: The moment he hit town, all the boys wanted to be his best buddy. But who did this paragon among boys choose as his friend? Me!

I remember the day I met him: I was at the tennis court when the whole troop of four or five American boys my age arrived on their bikes, and one of them was carrying Matt on the luggage rack over his rear fender. They all turned in unison, skidding to a gravel-spurting stop, hoping to impress the new kid. Matt's whole body wore a shrug. He surveyed the river, bemused. His sandy hair was long and straight, his features bluff and pleasant: Nothing special to see, and yet I felt a force. He cracked a joke and I doubled over laughing. My appreciation startled him, but then he joined me, gusting out a ready laugh in full enjoyment of his own joke, which had instantly become our joke. The other boys stood around with forced grins because they didn't get it. Suddenly, I tasted how it felt to be an insider. Matt and I were cool and these other guys wished they could be in with us.

A few days later, one of the other boys and I took Matt to Pebble Island. This was a small island in the Helmand River, bare of trees, just a whale-shaped mound of gravel swelling out of the water. It was only twenty feet from shore, and easy to wade to. Matt had a watermelon, so we took it along; it wasn't easy to lug it across the river, wading over slick stones with minnows and tadpoles flitting between our feet, particularly since we were carrying a couple of sharp kitchen knives, but we made it safely.

Once on land, we went to the far side of the island, carrying the big watermelon over the crest and down to the water's edge. The river was hundreds of feet across at that point, and four or five feet deep, yet the current was so swift, it braided the surface with ripples. About ten feet offshore, another little mound of gravel poked its head out of the water, a baby island. Matt suggested we eat our watermelon out there.

I remember staring across the thunderous current and wondering, Is there any reason to attempt this crossing? Yes, there were several. For one thing, it was waiting to be done. Then too, it might be fun. Third, we might not make it—always an incentive for boys. Fourth, it would be so cool if we made it. Fifth, our parents would disapprove. Sixth, gee, the water looked so tempting on a hot day like this, you could almost feel it around your legs, the cold and swift of it. Lots of reasons to get our enormous watermelon over to that little hump of gravel, actually. And let's not forget the most important reason of all. We were The Guys, pitting our banded strength against this awesome force of nature. I would never have tried it on my own, but when Matt suggested it, the redolence of pure adventure filled my lungs.

So we rolled up our pant legs, got the watermelon and

the knives firmly in hand, and waded into the water. And though it sucked at our ankles, piled up against our thighs, and threatened constantly to whoosh us away, we got there. Then Matt, the doctor's son, suggested that the watermelon was a critically ill patient and we were surgeons. We would have to operate at once. We got out our knives. We were looking at a delicate procedure; thank God we had the world-famous Dr. Matthew Murphy attending. We hunkered around him, watching the point of the knife slide into the tender green flesh and—

A horrendous shriek! Unbelievable! We'd forgotten to give the poor guy anesthetic! The watermelon struggled in our grasp, got away, rolled down toward the water, but we dived after it, saved the patient, dragged him back up to the operating table, where we sliced him open and cheerfully ate his innards, bleeding red juice down our chins under the sunlight, with the gorgeous Helmand roaring cold and wet around us, and I wondered if life would ever be this good again.

There were three girls in our age group in American Lashkargah: a toothy Texan named Linda, my quasi-sibling Rona Kayeum, and a future beauty queen named Elaine Simonson. I regarded all of them as pests until Matt brought me a whole new perspective.

"Elaine," he noted, "is hot. She wants my body."

I figured he was kidding. Goddesses do not want; they

are only wanted. But Matt openly chased Elaine, like some holy fool who believes he can grab the sun without burning his fingers. Then he stunned me with a further observation.

"But that Rona—phew!" He pretended to fan himself.

Huh? That putzy tattletale I'd more or less grown up with? That plump kid with the round face and the brown eyes and the big nose? "What about Rona?"

"That girl is *hot,* man! Mmmm-mm!"

I looked—and by God, he was right! *Rona Kayeum was a girl!*

The incredible discovery about Rona launched a friendly rivalry between Matt and me. We competed for Rona's favor by wrestling and punching each other in her presence. We fought for the seat next to hers at the Friday-night movies. We competed to dance with her at the socials. Every get-together ended with "Save the Last Dance for Me" and then a slow dance, and that's when our competition grew fierce as we jockeyed for position to get that precious last dance with Rona.

One Halloween, after a party at one of the American houses, Rona decided to let us both walk her home. Together, the three of us entered the Kayeum compound, passing the uniformed carbine-toting guard who stood watch in a booth at the gate. At her door, well within the compound walls, she said, "Okay, boys, each of you can give me one kiss," and she presented her cheek.

So we each stepped forward in turn and gave Rona

Kayeum a kiss, then skipped home, exulting over our feat and arguing about who had gotten the real kiss and who the mere mercy kiss. Such, then, was the American half of my divided life.

In my early childhood, Afghan women had to wear a *chad'ri* over their heads when they went out—a bag that came down to their ankles and offered only a mesh-covered peephole the size of a postcard to see through. But in 1959, the king's cousin, Prime Minister Daoud, called together the country's top religious scholars and said, "Here's the Koran. Show me where it says women must be veiled." They couldn't find the passage. Daoud thereupon declared the veil un-Islamic, and that year, at a public ceremony, the women of the royal family appeared with naked faces.

It's not that a law was changed. The *chad'ri* was a custom. But in 1959, the royal family made it their policy to oppose that custom. This was two years after we arrived in Lashkargah, and it fell to the HVA to sell the policy to the locals. My father and Kayeum decided to start by integrating the school. That's right, boys and girls would study together. To a student body of about 150 men and a smattering of boys was added one girl: my sister, Rebecca. It took courage and integrity for my father to put his own daughter on the line before asking anyone else to do so, but it put a heavy burden on Rebecca. On the appointed day, she donned a long black skirt, black stockings, and a white head scarf and walked the gauntlet into the tenth-grade classroom. The Afghan officials of Lashkargah winced and waited for the eruption of violence and rape.

Nothing happened, so the following week, Rona Kayeum came to our school. And the next day brought two more girls: the daughters of some clerks. But no one else took the plunge, and no one asked them to. More than a hundred males, and four females—two of them in my class.

One of them, Mahjoobah, was a classic Pashtun beauty: She had the thick black hair and the strong nose, the almond eyes, those high cheekbones and those full lips. No one at school dared to remark on her beauty, however. We boys never touched, talked to, or approached the girls. The two girls in our class—Mahjoobah and Amina—were seated in adjacent chairs at the front of the room, the far corner, in their batlike black outfits, quarantined from the rest of us by empty chairs.

Even so, coeducation enraged the conservative mullahs in Kandahar. One afternoon, I remember, my father took a phone call. His face turned pale as he listened, and his eyes turned as grim as I ever saw them. He hurried off to find Kayeum. It turned out that in Kandahar, a mob incited by the mullahs had gone on a rampage and killed some people. Kayeum alerted the government in Kabul by radio. Within hours, the government put tanks on the streets and jets in the air. Soldiers went house to house and squelched the rebellion. Only then did we learn that the outbreak had been part of a master plan. The whole province was supposed to rise up on the same day against the Westerners and the officials from Kabul. All of us in Lashkargah were supposed to have been killed. A few hotheads in Kandahar started early, and because of them, the plot failed and we survived.

Sometime after this, Mahjoobah asked Abdul Hadi for a pencil. Abdul Hadi was the handsome captain of my sister's tenth-grade classroom. Some said he gave Mahjoobah a pencil, though this was never proven. Some even claimed they had seen digit actually grazing against digit when the pencil changed hands. If so, went the buzz, who could guess what these two had going behind the scenes? The stories multiplied, until they got back to the authorities— to Kayeum, essentially. An assembly of the student body was called. No one told us what it was about (because any explanation would have entailed repeating the unspeakable rumors).

But certain fellows were called up to the platform one by one. Each was made to hold out his hand while a poplar branch was struck against his palm. The branch started out five or six feet long, but the slender tip kept breaking off and the beater kept moving in, beating with an ever-thicker handle, till the stick was too short to serve, at which point it was thrown away. That constituted "one stick" of beating, a standard unit of punishment. Some boys got two sticks; some even got three. Since we didn't know exactly why anyone was getting beaten, we didn't know whose name would be called next—although of course I and everyone else knew it wouldn't be me.

As I found out later, everyone thought to have repeated the improper rumor was beaten. Then the young men suspected of starting the stories were beaten. When the supposed ringleader, Malik Shah, a squat, pockmarked thug, was called to the podium, he had to remove his shoes. He was made to lie on the ground. Two guards grabbed his ankles and lifted him upside down, and then he got a *qufpayee,* a sole-of-the-footer. That is, the beater broke one stick, two sticks, three, four, five across his bare feet. Not till he began to whimper was he released to hobble back down among his fellows.

Were we done?

Not yet.

The worst offender had yet to get his deserts. This miscreant was Abdul Hadi himself, the subject of the rumors. No one intimated that he had started the story or behaved dishonorably, but as the subject of the scandal, he had to be punished. And apparently, etiquette, or protocol, or some such thing, demanded that he get a beating one stick worse than Malik Shah's. Hadi took his beating stoically, and never, to my knowledge, complained about it afterward. My father and Kayeum liked Hadi, and they were progressive-minded men; but in this matter of the rumor, they felt they had no choice but to set a swift example—because the mullahs of Kandahar were sharpening their knives and waiting for the king's men to slip up.

All the officials posted here from Kabul spoke Farsi, but the locals spoke Pashto, so classes were taught in Pashto. I had to learn this new language to keep up. Although I had tremendous educational advantages over the other students, books and opportunities they could hardly imagine, I never made valedictorian. At this school, we wrote no papers and got no credit for class participation. The rankings were established solely by exams given three times a year in each of our eighteen subjects. The exam periods lasted a week, and a student's grades in all subjects were added up to determine his or her class ranking.

Report cards were handed out at a big public ceremony attended by the town's officialdom. The rank of each student was announced as his or her name was called. If the student had failed, this, too, was stated: "Malik Shah—failure!"

Shortly after the Mahjoobah scandal and the subsequent beatings, we had our second triennial exams. In this period, only six boys and the two girls passed. (I came in second or third in the class, as usual.) Everyone else in the class failed, and the authorities droned out their names as usual at the big ceremony. One after another, the men or boys marched up, heads hanging sheepishly low after being loudly, publicly declared a FAILURE—and remember, these men had been dragged to the Lashkargah School by soldiers, and some had recently been beaten because they passed on the juicy rumor that "Abdul Hadi is hot for Mahjoobah."

One morning the following week, our class was allowed to take our chairs outside because the classroom was cold. We sat behind the quadrangle, out of sight of the principal's office. Our first-period teacher failed to show up that day for some reason, so we had a free hour. And then the many boys and men who had failed the exams got to jesting pugnaciously with the six of us who had passed.

The jesting got louder, cruder, more hostile. It dawned on me that we might be in trouble. It dawned on the other five, as well. We tried to move to a spot where the authorities would be able to see us, but the failures herded us back.

Malik Shah produced a long key chain, and at his signal, so did several others. The failures closed in on us, and then the beatings began. Let's say it was the longest class period of my life. At last, however, Malik Shah checked his watch and gave a signal, and the beatings stopped. The math teacher arrived, and the normal class routine resumed. I had welts under my clothes but no bad bruises on my face and no bleeding wounds. At home, I told some story about a rough soccer game. I had no desire to get my classmates in trouble. I just wanted to fit in.

UNINTENDED CONSEQUENCES

WHEN THE GOVERNMENT of Afghanistan decided to irrigate the desert, the administrators never intended for the water to bring up salt and ruin the soil, which caused the official government farms to fail. They fell afoul of the law of unintended consequences—apparently the one law in history you can really count on. It certainly governed our lives in that part of Afghanistan.

When the government built dams to tame the Helmand River, it did not take into account that remote villages downstream had developed intricate systems over the centuries, based on the river's erratic patterns. When the river's patterns suddenly grew regular, the ancient systems no longer worked. Those villages never knew why the river was flowing differently, only that their crops were failing. Unintended consequences.

When the government forced nomads to settle in towns and built schools like the one in Lashkargah, it didn't mean to produce a class of alienated young men who no longer fit into their rural villages. But they kept educating boys: Westernizing them, secularizing them, deculturing them; they kept churning out high school graduates, far more than the country's only university could accommodate, and graduating far more university students than the skin-thin technocracy could absorb. Blithely, they kept adding to a class of underemployed, semi-educated misfits looking for answers their culture couldn't give them. Unintended consequences.

As these leftovers morphed into potential troublemakers, the government, to get them off the streets, drafted them into an army whose officers had mostly been trained in the Soviet Union. So these alienated young men drifted into communism. Unintended consequences.

As these men finished their military service, the government tried to rid the capital of them by sending them to teach in rural schools. And so a cadre of Communists and potential Communists began to flourish across the land. Unintended consequences. The foot soldiers of the Communist parties that overthrew the monarchy in 1978 (with Soviet help) were guys like my classmates at the Lashkargah School, who had been beaten for repeating juicy rumors about sex.

Western aid pouring into Afghanistan transformed the cities but never touched the rural villages. So a gulf developed between sophisticated Kabul and the tribes. And when the Communists took over, they were oblivious to traditional Afghan society. The gulf became an ocean. Unintended consequences.

I've heard leftists describe the policies of the Afghan Communists with glowing terms like *land reform.* But land reform meant carving up lands under tribal control and giving the pieces to peasants from different tribes—as if they had more solidarity with one another than with their tribal kinfolk. But in Afghanistan, land is abundant; it's water that is scarce. Tribal control had produced and preserved communal arrangements for the use of water. Land reform meant water reform, too. Some peasants got an acre or two of land and just a trickle of water each week. Their crops failed. Unintended consequences.

The Communists promoted women's education. Their program meant jeeploads of soldiers roaring into rural villages and ordering the headmen to haul out the girls so that the soldiers could pick which ones to enroll in school. Tribal people, whose deepest emotions were vested in notions of honor and privacy, felt raped. Men and women could survive the assault, but the larger selves of which they were but the cells, those extended families, those clans, those tribes, felt not just their way of life threatened but also their very existence. And so they rose up against the outside power in rage and fear, determined not to die, and as those clans and tribes fought for survival, their cells died like ants in a war that demolished Afghan culture and shredded the social fabric over the next twenty-three years.

Unintended consequences? You can count on them.

LEAVING AFGHANISTAN

M Y FRIEND ROGER FRITZ went to a private high school in Colorado called CRMS—Colorado Rocky Mountain School—but he spent summer vacations with his family, which had moved to Lashkargah. In the summer of 1963, he told me that CRMS would give me a scholarship if I wrote to them. "They'd even pay your way to America," he said. "They did that for a couple of boys from Africa." It was a throwaway comment on his part, but it lodged in my brain like a worm.

I had big plans that summer. The swimming pool was back in operation and I hoped to better my record of swimming forty continuous laps. I had started on this project when the bombshell dropped.

The king seized power.

From whom does an absolute monarch seize power? Well, Zahir Shah (King Zahir) had been a figurehead ever since he was nineteen, when the assassination of his father put him on the throne. Normally, his adult uncles would have eliminated him and then fought among themselves, but the Mohammedzai uncles broke the pattern. They put the prince on the throne and took turns running the country as prime minister. Various royal relatives held all other top posts in the government. This civilized autocracy gave Afghanistan forty years of stability. King Zahir, formerly the prince, got to live in a palace, ride in a Rolls-Royce, and take vacations in Italy. But he did not get to order troops into battle, set policy vis-à-vis Pakistan, or go eyeball-to-eyeball with the Soviet ambassador.

When the last uncle died, the king's cousin Daoud took charge, and this must have chafed. The king was getting on toward fifty, and no doubt he wanted to be a real king at last. And then Daoud screwed up. He forced a macho showdown with Pakistan over a border dispute—and lost. When he backed down, Afghanistan lost face. This gave Zahir Shah an opening.

The king moved swiftly to fire his cousin and all the rest of his relatives. He announced that he was launching Afghanistan on a path to democracy. He convened a committee of "wise men" (including my uncle Najmuddin) to draft a new constitution, and they came up with a document that *prohibited*—strong language!—any member of the royal family from holding any cabinet-level post in government. Henceforth, only commoners could hold these posts.

In 1963, the king accepted this constitution, which then

became the law of the land. Commoners like Dr. Kayeum and my father had been groomed to administer the country. Now they were being invited to step up and rule it. The Western-educated technocrats began jockeying for power.

My father did not get in on the jockeying. He was in the United States on government business at the time, and his best friend did not save him a seat at the show. The scrambling must have been intense, and Kayeum no doubt had his hands full securing his own seat. Nonetheless, when my father returned to Afghanistan and discovered that all his friends had moved up and he was an unemployed has-been, he felt betrayed.

His "best friend," Dr. Abdul Kayeum, was now Minister of Interior. In Afghanistan (as in most Third World countries), this ministry did not concern itself with recreation and parks. It was in charge of keeping the "interior" under control. It mirrored the foreign portfolio. The minister appointed governors, operated the police force, and conducted diplomacy with the ever-dangerous tribes. A comparable office in the United States would run the state governments, the National Guard, and the FBI. On paper, then, Kayeum was roughly the fifth-most-powerful man in Afghanistan.

Kayeum promised to get my father a post in the Ministry of Interior, and he did, a few months later, but not the post my father expected—that of deputy minister. My father got a job one rung lower down, director of administration or some such.

His government-issue car served as a visible emblem of

his fall. Cabinet ministers and their deputies each got a Mercedes. We got a clunky cast-iron Soviet-made Volga. We were Volga-class officials now. It could have been worse. We could have gotten a Moscovitz, the Soviet version of a Ford Escort. Or no car at all. Or we could have fallen out of government service altogether, back into Neolithic Afghanistan.

But I could only see what we weren't. My teenage years in Afghanistan were dominated by the shame of my father's fall, even though in truth he was not such a failure. He was four tiers down from ruling the country, maybe five. What did I want of him—that he lead a coup d'état? I don't know.

My father's appointment meant we had to move back to Kabul. Our quasi-American life in Lashkargah was over. My mother was depressed. We children were depressed. At the last of several going-away parties, Rona cast off all pretense of doling out her favors equally and chose Matt, clinging to him during the last dance. I was not jealous. It was Matt I loved—our camaraderie, our trips to the island, our explorations of the ruined city, our swimming competitions at the pool. Competing for Rona was just an element in our great friendship, now ending.

We returned to the family compound with the nine-foot walls. It seemed so much smaller now, prisonlike. I enrolled in a Kabul high school, the one situated next to the Royal Palace. Most of the upper-class families sent their sons there—the various branches of the royal family and those commoners who had risen to the level of cabinet minister. Among them, I felt humiliated because we had sunk to Volga-class status.

Istiqlal was the second-oldest school in Afghanistan and still in its original plant, a standard Afghan compound: a ring of rooms surrounding a courtyard hidden from the public eye. The classrooms smelled of mold and must, and the floors were of worn, uneven brick. Each of the Kabul high schools had been built by a different Western country—two by the United States, one by Germany, and this one, Istiqlal, by France.

All the scientific and technical classes at Istiqlal—math, physics, chemistry, and the like—were taught by Frenchmen, in French. Another new language! I studied nothing but French for six months. Only then could I attend regular Istiqlal classes. We sat in the familiar rows of two-person desks. My seatmate, Humayun, was fond of sexual innuendo and often tried teasingly to feel me up. Once, he pulled his homework out of his notebook clumsily and a chunk tore out of the middle. When I suggested that the teacher might not like this, he winked at me and said, "I'll just tell him, 'But Teacher-sir, every one of God's creatures has a hole.'" I had to laugh in disbelief that he'd found a way to put a sexual slant on even this trivial situation.

That year, the government decided to follow up on the Lashkargah experiment and move toward coeducation in the Kabul schools. Our school was chosen as the testing ground. Again they started slowly, with just two girls. One was the daughter of a Madame Shukoor, a French woman married to an Afghan. The other was good old Rona

Kayeum again. There they sat, in our classroom at Istiqlal, wearing the regulation outfit: black dress, black stockings, white head scarf, gloves, the works.

In all the months those girls were in my class, only once did I hear words exchanged between them and any boy. I remember the occasion clearly. The French-Afghan girl (I don't remember her name) approached a clump of boys and said, "Does anyone have a pencil I can use?"

A pencil, for God's sake! Of all things for her to request! But there was no eruption of sexual humor. Although I'm sure these boys knew nothing of the episode in Lashkar-gah, they knew not to treat intergender stuff in the public realm lightly. Not in that era, not in Afghanistan. With great ceremony and utmost tact, my seatmate, Mr. Sexual Innuendo himself, walked up the aisle to the front of the room and placed a pencil on the arm of a chair, where she could pick it up after he had sat down again.

Such was coeducation in Afghanistan. But here's the thing. When I got home, I'd go over to the Kayeums'; they lived down the block from us again. Rona and I would discuss the day at school, laugh at the religion teacher. I'd tell her who was who among the boys: We were friends, and with a sexual tingle.

Two systems. The mind cannot contain both as legitimate. That's my testimony. When you're in two worlds so different, your mind is forced to say that one is legitimate and the other is a crock.

My mind chose the American ethos as legitimate. Why? Because it promised more fun? I don't know. I do know, however, that on this issue of sex, Afghanistan and I parted ways. And parting ways on this, we parted ways on everything. I'll go out on a limb and say that I think it is on this issue of sex and the relationship between the sexes that Islam and the West have parted ways, and parting ways on this, have parted ways on everything.

One day, application forms arrived from CRMS. I went out to the back yard and gazed at jagged mountains far away. Growing up, I had dreamed of living alone in the mountains when I came of age. It amounted to a spiritual yearning—an intense desire to be part of all that naked beauty. Now, the idea of going to America had that same quality—that same intensity and sweetness, that same "Is this actually possible?" feel. Could I, Tamim Ansary, son of a Volga-class Afghan official, actually live in America someday? I just couldn't tell.

Nervously, I filled out the application. As it happened, my parents were already busy working out a way to send my sister Rebecca to college in the United States. They'd found an option in Kentucky, at a college called Berea, which would basically be free if she could get in.

When I told my parents about my CRMS scheme, they thrummed with hope. After twenty years in Afghanistan, my mother wanted to return to America. And that whole business with the Volga-class job had left my father angry and embittered. He was ready to consider a move. My parents told me that if I could get a scholarship to CRMS, they'd somehow rustle up the airfare.

The day the letter of acceptance arrived from CRMS, I told Humayun I was going to America on a high school scholarship. He stood up in math class that day and announced the news to the whole class. The teacher, a Frenchman famous for slapping misbehaving students with a limp hand—the boys said it felt like a sack of boneless meat—just stared at me and said, "*Très bien. Bonne chance.*"

Another few months would pass before I left for America, but after that day, the classes, the boys, the courtyard, the willow trees, the soccer games, the homosexual innuendos, all grew curiously fantastic, as if Afghanistan was losing its reality for me while I was still in the middle of it.

Sometime in those last days, Madame Shukoor invited our family to a party. We'd never had much truck with French-Afghans, but we recognized them to be part of that charmed otherworld, the West. The Kayeums were invited, too, and so were about a dozen other Afghan-European families. After dinner, one room was cleared of furniture, and we young people danced to rock 'n' roll records. Madame Shukoor's daughter was wearing a red cashmere sweater and a skirt that ended at her knees, leaving her legs bare. All that school year, I had seen her only out of the corner of my eye, garbed in bat black and covered with a head shawl. Never had I forgotten myself so utterly as to meet her eyes. Now suddenly she was a vibrant, hot-blooded female; we were dancing and trading repartee; she was letting me hold her close during slow numbers. It wasn't lust that I felt; it was passionate romantic love. Needless to say, I never set eyes on her again.

Late one night, a Mr. Green from the American embassy knocked on the door of our compound. My father let him in. He hurried furtively across the yard and to the house, a blond man in a long khaki coat. He was carrying a bulky briefcase. We pulled shut the burlap curtains in the living room, turned off the lights, and lit candles so no one could peep in at us. Then he opened the briefcase and produced the dangerous document hidden within: the U.S. Constitution.

My mother, it turned out, had discovered she was still an American citizen. She had never lost her citizenship, because she had never renounced it. And when we kids were born, she had gone to the U.S. embassy and quietly registered our births, never really knowing why. As a result, however, we could now be U.S. citizens, too, just by swearing an oath.

Mr. Green set the Constitution on the dining room table; we raised our hands in the candlelight and swore to uphold the laws of the United States. Then he handed us our passports. I felt like one of those peasants in the fairy tales who discover that they are actually princes who were given away at birth to protect them from some evil spell. Now that we had come of age, we could claim our rightful inheritance. We were Americans after all!

My father was there, but he didn't get a passport, of

course, because he certainly wasn't an American citizen, but I didn't think we were leaving him behind. I assumed he would be staying in Kabul only long enough to tie up the loose ends of his affairs. Then he would follow us to America, where we would all be together as a family again.

And later, in America, when people asked if my parents were separated, I always said no, except for the fact that she was in America and he in Kabul. After our departure, my father's fortunes turned around in Afghanistan. He jumped to the Mercedes level of government official by receiving the post he coveted, Deputy Minister of Interior. But he gave it up and followed us to America. He took the very junior position of press attaché at the Afghan embassy in Washington, D.C., a job far beneath his age and status, in order to live with us.

The job didn't even last a whole year, however. The government in Kabul went through some upheaval, and a faction unfriendly to my father came to power. They stripped him of his job by abolishing his position. I was away at school when this happened, but my brother was home. And I learned many years later that when my father broke the news about his job at the dinner table, my brother burst out crying. He was only nine or so, but he knew what this meant. He knew it meant that my father was going to leave us, and that our family, so recently joined together, would be torn asunder.

And that's just what happened. The Kabul government ordered my father to come home, whereupon he faced a decision. Should he obey his orders or stay in America with us? His American option was to apply for a position as professor of Persian literature in an American university. All summer, he kicked around the apartment morosely, doing crossword puzzles and trying to decide. I had no sympathy for his anguish. I had just finished my junior year at Colorado Rocky Mountain School and was busy exploring college options. Big school or little? Urban or small-town locale? Classical education or one of those free-form new schools springing up? Now, those were some tough decisions, in my opinion.

My father's situation struck me as a no-brainer. A college professor—what a great life! What was the problem?

Only later did I realize that my father was not fundamentally agonizing over his job prospects. In his mid-forties by then, he felt a dreadful finality about the choice. If he went back, he might never get out again: He would lose us. If he stayed, he might never be allowed into Afghanistan again: He would lose his larger family, his brothers, the clan—that greater self to which an Afghan belongs by birthright.

In the end, he chose the larger family. Without them, I think, he felt he wouldn't exist. I was away at school when he took off, so I never did say good-bye to my father, and I certainly didn't say it or even think it the night Mr. Green gave us our passports.

I never said a real good-bye to my relatives in Afghanistan, either, because we weren't supposed to be leaving forever.

The Afghan government didn't consider us to be Americans. To them, we were Afghans, since our father was an Afghan and since we children were born in Afghanistan. Officially, therefore, we would be returning at some point. My father completed the paperwork and bribed the necessary bureaucrats to get us Afghan passports.

We arrived at the airport with our American passports hidden in our baggage. At the gate, we showed our Afghan passports and travel documents. Even the other Ansarys thought that my sister and I were going abroad to study and that my mother and eight-year-old brother were coming along just to get us settled. Our departure from Afghanistan was actually a defection—an escape. The plane took off and I watched the terminal receding below. About leaving Afghanistan, I felt nothing. I only felt sorry to be separated from that girl in the red cashmere sweater. I fell asleep fantasizing that we would meet again someday in the United States . . . where we could date. . . .

The next thing I knew, we were landing in Tehran and our journey to the West had truly begun. Soon I would be relieved of the discomforts of a divided self, free to roam the world as just one person: Tamim Ansary, American guy.

PART TWO

·

Looking for Islam

THE LETTER

DURING MY FATHER'S MONTHS in Washington, we were connected to a network of Afghans, but after he left, those connections faded, and we didn't try to hold on to them. Fourteen years passed, during which I never met another Afghan and never had occasion to speak Farsi, which was just fine with me. I finished high school and college and weathered ruinous love affairs. Then I plunged into the counterculture in Portland, Oregon, where I was living at this time.

To my American friends, the counterculture was an extension of college life. For me, it had an additional resonance, one I didn't recognize explicitly at the time. The tribal pretensions of the counterculture spoke to my Afghan soul. In Portland, I was part of an intimate community—we sometimes even called ourselves a tribe—a closely interwoven network of friends and lovers numbering perhaps two hundred, just about the size of the Ansary network in Kabul and Deh Yahya.

We spent much of our time just being with our group. Very Afghan. We lived in various communal houses scattered about the city; to me, they were like the Ansary compounds in the hidden urban village of my childhood. Our doors were always open to others of our network, and we thought nothing of hanging out by ourselves in one another's living rooms. The counterculture had that familiar feeling of a warm world nested within and hidden from the public realm. Strangers had no idea who we really were, and we walked among them with caution. Only upon arriving safely indoors—any indoors in our communal network—did we let down our guard.

When I finally started to swim out of the counterculture in 1976, I had been away from Afghanistan for twelve years but had never really lived in America yet. That year, I cut my hair, traded in my wild hippie garb for corduroys and sport shirts, and moved to San Francisco, where I got my first real job. I wanted to be a writer, but I ended up editing a newspaper for an outfit called the Asia Foundation, which financed tiny development projects in various Asian countries.

As soon as I got to San Francisco, I went looking for a communal living situation, and my quest soon brought me to 1049 Valencia. The first roommate I saw when I knocked on the door for my interview was Debby Krant. I still remember her standing at the top of the stairs, silhouetted against the faint light from another room, short and bouncy, with big cheeks and an irrepressible grin. She made her living as a clown, I learned, in a children's theater troupe called Make-a-Circus, where she was known as Brunetta the Dancing Bear.

My interview went well. Debby and the other two women at the house liked me and I liked them. As soon as I moved in, my life became splendidly American. I was young, I had a steady income, my job was stimulating, and my roommates adorable. I had no obligations. I could go out every night if I felt like it, and I felt like it every night. I fancied myself an artist, and my friends endorsed my fancy. By day, working at the Asia Foundation, I hobnobbed with important people in suits. After work, I knocked about socially with paint-spattered lowlifes who plotted revolution and wrote plays.

Most of all, I finally began to figure out this unusual American custom called dating, in which unrelated strangers meet and explore the possibility of a sexual relationship. It wasn't hard once you got the hang of it. For a while, I dated as energetically as that cliché, the divorced man with a Porsche, except that I didn't have a Porsche and had never been married; indeed, I regarded marriage as an outmoded bourgeois concept.

Then one morning in October 1979, Debby brought the mail upstairs and handed me an envelope from *Gourmet* magazine. To my astonishment, it contained a check for one thousand dollars. The stub said this check was payment for an article about Afghan cuisine, and indeed I had sent such a piece to *Gourmet* long ago, but they had never responded, even to my follow-up queries. Now, a year and a half later, without explanation or cover letter, this whopping check dropped out of the sky. (And I might add that no explanation ever followed, nor was the article ever published.)

The unexpected check handed me an ultimatum. I had a long-standing plan to go on a major trip someday. The seed had been planted in 1972, when I met a man who had just come home from travels in North Africa and Asia. He told me he'd done some of his best bumming around in Afghanistan, in those sociable bazaars that I remembered so well: He talked about eating *jilabi* and fried fish, and riding those multicolored lorries through Herat and Kandahar and Ghazni. He talked about Kabul, where he'd lingered for a month, marveling at the mixture of sophistication and isolation, the big-city air combined with the utter remoteness of the place.

At that point, Afghanistan was still so recent in my past that I could picture it without having to fill in from the imagination, and yet distant enough that I no longer felt the bicultural alienation of my childhood. I could remember and respect and even nostalgically long for the pride that was mine in that society as an Ansary, and the love that was my unquestioned harvest within the walls of any Ansary compound. So this fellow's account of his travels overwhelmed me with desire. I asked how much the whole trip had cost and he said three thousand dollars. I promised myself at once that if I ever had three thousand dollars in the bank, I'd head for Asia.

The check from *Gourmet* brought my savings to just about three thousand dollars.

But was I bound by that promise to myself? My brain began to wheedle. I had so many reasons to stay in San Francisco right then.

Well, okay, I had only one reason. I had fallen in love with Brunetta the Dancing Bear, my circus clown of a roommate. It sneaked up on me gradually, almost imperceptibly. We crossed paths every night when we got home, and she was always there when I went down for breakfast. I began to notice I was having no trouble getting up in the morning. As soon as I drifted to that early-morning place where sleep gets wispy, I remembered the existence of Debby and felt happy. The prospect of making coffee together, of our morning chitchat, of her reading items from the newspaper out loud to me while I strained to concentrate on "Doonesbury" and the sports news, she in her black floor-length housedress, intimations of her soft body bulging the cloth out here and there, the ease of the whole occasion . . . added up to one distinct pleasure I could count on if only I could make it out of bed by ten of eight.

I never thought the friendship was building toward anything, because I knew that sex with a roommate was verboten. It's true that in the Portland counterculture, we sought romance only with others in our intimate network of close friends, but I understood that I had entered a different culture now. This was America. I was to look for romances outside the house, and I did. And so did she, which set us free to relax in each other's company. We became not only best friends but confidants in matters of the heart.

One day, an ex-girlfriend blew into town, a girl who had left me in college, and about whom I had been obsessing ever since. She and I spent a day together now, and she opened her heart to me in the way I had been craving for years; yet right in the middle of my enjoyment, I found myself swamped by an utter *longing* to go home—and why? To tell Debby.

At home, the whole gang was on the back porch, barbecuing chicken. The fridge bristled with cold beers. Debby was there with her boyfriend of the time, but I wasn't jealous. I was floating in a happiness hard to define—it had something to do with being in the privacy of my hidden world, back in the compound. But the focal point of my happiness was Debby. Who was like my relative. Who was like a cousin to me. And Afghans, you may remember, prefer to marry their cousins.

But I never allowed myself to entertain erotic thoughts about Debby. I only allowed myself—fatally, as it turned out—to admire her many good qualities. She was so directed. So competent. So patient and positive. She never gave way to spite or petty vengeance . . . never made excuses for herself.

Each time I spotted another of these virtues, I thought, I wish I could find someone like Debby in *that* way. It took months for me to admit to myself finally that what I wanted was Debby herself. But we were roommates . . . locked into this accursed confidant thing—how to change the footing?

Sometimes when we sat at the dining room table exchanging confidences, I felt like we were living in the tropics, the temperature climbed so high. Debby never seemed to notice. "How are things with Annabelle?" she would ask innocently about my latest romance.

And I, spotting an opening, would say, "It isn't going to last. You see, Debby, the kind of woman I *really* want—"

But she would cut me short. She always treated me like a punch-drunk boxer who needed a wet towel and encouragement to get back in the fray. "Give Annabelle a chance," she advised me warmly. "Relationships need time to grow."

Clearly, with Debby, I would have to limit myself to admiration of her solid virtues.

But admiration of solid virtues such as patience can intensify to an erotic pitch. Indeed they can. Slowly, the knowledge came to permeate my cells that all my millions of selves wanted only for the gates to open so we could rush with glad abandon into the crowded millions of her selves, shaking hands, hugging, and rolling on the grass until we were wholly intermingled.

And that's where matters stood the day I received one thousand dollars from *Gourmet*. I didn't want to go anywhere. But should I break a solemn promise to myself to stay near a woman who had no inkling of my feelings and never would?

I did, after all, have solid reasons to go. One was my career—or lack thereof. The Iranian revolution had erupted that year, setting off a frenzy among American journalists. A mass movement had overthrown Shah Mohammed Reza Pahlavi, the king of Iran. Although it included student activists of every stripe, the movement was dominated by religious and cultural conservatives led by that austere and ferocious old buzzard, the Ayatollah Khomeini. Khomeini and his followers declared Iran an Islamic state, and no one quite knew what that meant. In the West, indeed, most people had only the vaguest notions of Islam itself, and the papers were full of articles purporting to "educate" the public about this religion. These stories always dwelled on the punishments prescribed in the *sharia,* the Islamic legal code—thieves should have their hands cut off; liars should have their tongues ripped out; adulterers should be stoned. . . .

But I had grown up in the most purely Islamic society of modern times, and I had never heard of a hand being chopped off, a tongue being ripped out, or an adulterer being stoned. I wondered if I might not break into a career as a macho journalist by traveling through the Islamic world and writing the real story of Islam. I had the money to do it now, and who was better equipped to get that story?

I went to see a little outfit called the Pacific News Service. The year before, when the Communists seized control of Afghanistan, I had sold them a "think piece" predicting the fall of Iran. Now that Iran had fallen, my stock was running high with the folks at PNS, and so I pitched them my idea about traveling through the Islamic world.

The intellectual godfather of PNS listened with inter-

est. He was a mild-mannered, snowy-haired, left-leaning
Berkeley history professor named Franz Schurmann.
Schurmann believed that Islam had revolutionary appeal
because it addressed the economic needs of the poor—by
emphasizing alms and the malefactions of great wealth, I
guess. Neither capitalism nor Marxism had managed to alleviate poverty, so people were looking for another option.
If you peered through the surface rhetoric, the religious
tenets, all the talk about One God versus the Christian
Trinity, you'd find the same factors driving this revolution
as every other revolution: hunger, poverty, disease, thirst,
colonial oppression, and so on. In other words, Marxist
theory predicted this resurgence of Islam. Schurmann said
he'd be glad to publish pieces from the field that illustrated
his thesis. I agreed on the spot, because his thesis sounded
so obvious. I figured the pieces would practically write
themselves.

I had one further reason for this journey, which I'll get
to later, but I didn't need one further reason: The response
from PNS clinched it. If this trip would give me the opportunity to write for money and accumulate clips, I really
had no choice. I told my friends about my decision; and at
that point I began confessing to all and sundry, except
our immediate roommates, that I had fallen in love with
Debby. Why hide it anymore? I announced frankly that if I
broke through with her before I left, I would return. If not,
I would say good-bye forever. My men friends rolled their
eyes at this and changed the subject to football. My women
friends thought it was all so thrillingly romantic. My clos-

est friend, however, had no opinion—this friend being, of course, Debby. She was the last to know.

But then at last, she knew, too. It came out during our annual 1049 Valencia Street Halloween party. Four of us lived in this house, and since we had nonoverlapping circles of friends, and our friends had friends who told their friends, our annual party had been burgeoning every year. In 1979, it reached monstrous proportions. It became a virtual public party. By nine o'clock, our enormous two-story flat brimmed with strangers. By ten, it was full of raging drunks. By eleven, the place looked like a cross between the bar in *Star Wars* and a setting from a Fellini movie. Debby was dressed as Medusa that night. She had green snakes coming out of her head. I was the Incredible Two-Headed Transplant and had an extra head sprouting out of my turtleneck. She was dancing flirtatiously with someone, and I couldn't take it anymore. I strode across the dance floor, crowded that poor guy out of the way, and said, "Stop. I can't bear this. I'm jealous."

Her face grew pale right through her green Medusa makeup. "You can't feel that way!" she gasped. "You're like my brother."

"I can't help how I feel," I cried, "and besides, I'm not—technically speaking—when you get right down to it—*actually*—your brother." More like a cousin, I was thinking: a perfect match.

"I can't deal with this." She fled from me, vanishing among witches and gypsies, dead presidents, and Elvis impersonators. I ran after her, squeezing between two Chewbaccas and a naked woman, brushing past Nixon in drag, up the stairs and through the crowded hall to her closed bedroom door. I knocked but got no answer. "Dude," said some lout in the hall, "she's *with* someone. Be cool!"

I staggered out of my own party and walked the streets, distraught. Someplace out in the dark, I ran into my old friend Paul Lobell, who took me to a nearby dough-nut shop patronized exclusively by junkies, hookers, and pimps. He poured me full of coffee, sympathized with my tale, and got me home.

The next day, Debby and I couldn't look each other in the eye because we were brimming with flood-scale emo-tions. All week, these feelings kept rising behind our dams of feigned indifference. Unbeknownst to me, she was see-ing a therapist that week, trying to cope with her guilt about the incestuous feelings I had triggered in her. Finally, the therapist said, "Well, *is* this man your brother?" And Debby had to admit that no, I wasn't.

On November 3—the day before my birthday—I went to a travel agent and with grim despair bought a ticket to the East Coast. That same day, I quit my job. I was like those guys who do the luge: in the ice chute now, no turn-ing back.

Then it was November 4—my birthday. I turned thirty-one that day. Around noon, Debby came to me and asked tremulously if I wanted to go out with her that night to celebrate. "Go out?" I said. "Just you and me?" Shakily, she said yes. It didn't matter where we went. Almost randomly, we ended up at a club called the Hotel Utah, where a heavy-metal transvestite band called Doris Fish and the Sluts a-Go-Go were playing. We scarcely noticed them; we were too busy not looking at each other, and then looking at each other, and then the dams were crumbling and we went home, and before the night was out, we were no longer just roommates.

I had broken through with the love of my life, but the trip was still on. In one week, I was going to leave her and head off to the ends of the earth. Then we turned on the TV and saw the news, and I thought, Oh man. *This* can't be good for my trip. A bunch of radical Iranian students had stormed the American embassy in Tehran that day and taken fifty-three Americans hostage.

THE CONVERT

I HAD TO GO TO WASHINGTON to get my visas in order. My mother still lived in the Maryland suburbs. When she returned to the United States, she came with no job and little money, a middle-aged woman with virtually no résumé in America. Fortunately, before destitution overtook her, she found a teaching job in Harriman, Tennessee. This Bible Belt town was not a congenial place for a twenty-year atheist veteran of Islamic Afghanistan. She just taught her classes and holed up in her tiny rental, lonely and frightened, with only my brother Riaz for company. Kindly neighbors kept trying to enroll her in their churches, but she told them she had joined another congregation elsewhere in town. When my father got his embassy job, she moved gratefully to Washington, D.C.

She had a limited social life after he left. Somehow, after all those years in Afghanistan, she didn't know how to wade back into American society. She never remarried, never divorced my father, never went out on a date, and never had a boyfriend again. And she didn't have many friends. She went to work as an elementary school teacher, and that's where she put all the love left over from the considerable portion she budgeted for us children. I didn't know she even had any love left over. I thought she just did the teaching job as a grinding chore. Not till she was in her eighties and her memory was failing did I realize how much teaching had meant to her. I was writing a column on what makes a teacher great and I decided to ask her opinion. "With the younger children," she said, "you have to love them. I did a lot of smiling as a teacher. I smiled at them in the halls, I smiled at them in the classroom, so they would feel safe. You have to make every child the center of your attention."

I scoffed at that one. "Every child can't be the center of your attention—by definition," I pointed out.

"Yes," she insisted. "They can."

At this point, she was fuzzy on which were my children and which my brother's, but she was still reading stories to children as a classroom volunteer. I went with her to one such session. I watched this frail old woman, nearly deaf and wheezing with emphysema, gingerly take her place in the reader's chair—but the moment she was seated with a book in her hand and surrounded by children, her demeanor changed. Suddenly, she was masterful. She interacted with the children as she read, asked them questions, directed their attention, defused little situations. As soon as the reading was done, she struggled off the chair, a helpless old woman again.

In 1980, the night I arrived in Maryland, my mother and I went out to dinner, as we always did. She wanted to split the check. I couldn't believe my ears. The rule had always been: If I could reach her apartment even one inch ahead of the hounds of poverty, I could flop and recuperate for free, eating well and sleeping late, as long as I wanted. She was my mother, after all!

"Maybe you don't realize this," I said between clenched teeth, "but I'm a little tense about money right now."

"So am I," she said.

Oh—she wanted to compare poverty? "Well," I forced out, "I'm about to set off on a long journey with three thousand dollars, and I've already spent two hundred of it and I'll have to drop another three hundred just to get to Europe. If I run out somewhere in the world, I might be stranded. That's what I'm tense about. What are you tense about?"

She said, "I'm reaching the end of my rope with teaching. I'm old. Every year, the kids get more difficult to control. I didn't work in the United States till I was forty. I haven't got much in my retirement and nothing built up in my Social Security. I don't think I've got the strength to keep working much longer, but I don't think I can afford to retire. That's what I'm tense about."

Then my brother Riaz arrived home from Pakistan. He was the "one further reason" I mentioned earlier—perhaps the main reason I was setting off on this journey.

Riaz was seven years younger than I, and I had always felt as much parental as fraternal toward him—he was my darling, my sweet, my adored little brother! I could remember him at the age of one minute—a wrinkled bag of featureless pink skin, *such* a disappointment after the months of anticipation Rebecca and I had gone through, and yet . . . strangely fetching. And I remember once when he was about a year old, he was lying on a bed and I was jumping on the bed to make him bounce, jumping high and landing hard, with my feet straddling his powdered little pink body.

On one of those *boings,* little Riaz burst into laughter! Perhaps he had laughed elsewhere, earlier, unbeknownst to me, but the sound of his sudden squeals exhilarated me like unexpected air under wings I never knew I had. I believed and still believe that I taught my brother to laugh.

He didn't laugh much in the years that followed. His real parent in Lashkargah was a white-bearded old relative of ours named Mawmaw, who was living with us. When Riaz was about six, we discovered that Mawmaw was stealing from us. My mother sent the old rascal packing, back to the village. How dismayed Riaz must have been to discover that one of his three parents could be fired by the other two. When Riaz was eight, we left Afghanistan, left my father. When Riaz was nine, my father left America, left us. After that, Riaz grew up alone with my mother, a middle-aged loner who clung to him as virtually her entire social world.

But I was the one who had given Riaz the idea of going

to Pakistan—as inadvertently as I had taught him how to laugh. One day, I was blabbing to him about some plan to learn welding, get a welding job, save some money, and go close enough to Afghanistan to gaze across the border. I couldn't actually go in, because the king had fallen and his cousin Daoud had set up a military dictatorship. Besides, the Afghan government was waiting to draft me as soon as I stepped inside, which would have cost me my American citizenship. But the symbolism of standing on the border and gazing across—yes, I wanted that.

The next time I saw Riaz, he was in welding school in Washington State; the time after that, he was telling me how much money he'd saved; and the time after that, asking me for a ride to the freeway so he could hitchhike to New York and board a plane for Pakistan. When I dropped him at the ramp and watched him walk away from me in the rain, I felt anxoius: My delicate little brother was only twenty, scarcely old enough to live on his own—how could he possibly make it all the way to Pakistan and back? His skin was so pale, his hair so blond—what if someone in a refugee camp mistook him for a Russian? What if he never came back?

After a few months, I got a letter from him. The big news was that he had "embraced Islam." I figured it was just a phase. After all, he was my *brother*—a longhaired, intellectual college guy, serious about art, serious about environmental issues, serious about a lot of things—and thoroughly rational in his approach to life. But the letters kept coming, and he kept writing about the "light" he saw in the faces of the Peshawar Pashtuns. I got to wondering what he had found over there. And if he had been converted, could I be converted, too?

Now, here he was at Friendship Airport, wearing his long Pakistani shirt over his loose Pakistani trousers and sporting a skullcap. From his chin hung the best beard he could manage, a thin collection of very long hairs.

He had embraced an orthodox interpretation of Islam, I discovered, and over the next week, I learned just how many details this interpretation entailed. When he unpacked, his kit included a twig with a frayed end, which is called a *maswak;* it's what Prophet Muhammad had brushed his teeth with. Apparently, Riaz's new religious views precluded the use of a normal toothbrush. He would not sleep on a bed, only on the floor. At meals, he insisted on eating with his hands.

And of course he said his prayers at the appointed times, no matter where he was, for which reason he always carried a watch, a compass, and a prayer rug. One day, we were riding a bus when the prayer hour arrived. Riaz checked his compass. When the bus hit a long straightaway pointed toward Mecca, he rolled that prayer rug out in the aisle and moved into the prayer position. He didn't care that people were sniggering and pointing. He seemed almost to relish enduring some ridicule for his new faith. And it was all my fault: I had inspired him to go to Pakistan.

As a Muslim, Riaz had many special needs. For example, he could only eat meat that was *halal,* meat from an approved animal slaughtered according to scriptural provisions—by having its throat slit while God's name was invoked as it took its dying breath. Nothing at the local supermarket fit these criteria.

We heard about a local Maryland farm catering to Muslims, where a person could buy a lamb and slaughter it personally. We drove out there the next Saturday. The place had a run-down look. An old car with flat tires sat rusting in the yard. The weathered fence bore a sign threatening in loud letters DOG WILL BITE! A big yellow hound came bounding across the dusty yard, wagging its tail and lolling its tongue. Riaz got out of the car, his loose white Muslim clothes rippling in the slight breeze. I followed him, indistinctly American in my running shoes, Levi's, and sweatshirt, bareheaded and with medium-length hair.

The farm woman waved to us from the house. "That dog won't bite you!" she said scornfully. "Drive on in."

From her yard, we could see about twenty animals, goats and lambs, penned up behind a shed. In the yard, a few dozen semi-bald chickens scratched in the dirt around our feet. Suddenly, the hound came hurling into the flock, snapping left and right, and the chickens scattered, then returned, missing a few more feathers, and started pecking miserably at the dirt again. I went into the farmhouse to pay for the lamb we intended to take, while my brother went into the animal pen.

The farm boy was stropping a foot-long butcher knife to a gleaming edge.

From the pen, Riaz called out, "Hey, Tamim! Come

help me pick one out." I joined him, wondering what help he could possibly need. The animals stood staring at us from a distance. Up to this moment, I had been looking at them as meat, but with their eyes upon me, I felt ashamed. Whichever one I pointed to would die, and they all knew it somehow. "That one," I said with a vague gesture.

"This one?" The boy moved, but the goats and lambs scattered like minnows. I saw that I couldn't get away with gesturing at whole bunches of them; I would have to sentence a specific animal to death. I lunged and caught one, and the farm boy snatched its legs out and brought it crashing to earth, where the lamb lay quietly then, blinking and waiting. The other animals stirred uneasily but kept their distance. Only the yellow hound remained cheerful, chasing through the herd. The farm boy and I held down the sheep's legs and Riaz lifted its chin to expose its throat.

Then he started cutting through the hide. The lamb jerked in terror, but we stifled its struggle. The blood came spurting out, and Riaz kept sawing doggedly until he had cut about halfway through the sheep's neck. All the other animals had gathered around us, riveted by the drama; I could feel their shocked stares like the spokes of a wheel. The dog lapped eagerly at the bright blood. The sheep started to kick and kept on kicking, and I just held on, feeling the life ebbing out of its limbs. Riaz was frantically muttering the necessary Arabic syllables, which clacked from his tongue like cold marbles; his lips looked blue against his white face.

The lamb let out a last long asthmatic hiss. "Good enough," the farm boy declared, and he jumped up. We helped him drag the sheep to a shed, where he set to work sawing it up into chops and cuts and slabs. Riaz went off to perform his ablutions and say his prayers. I just stood by the car, feeling a fearful divergence between us, a divergence beyond words. Killing the lamb had shaken him, but it had not dented his resolve, which was steelier than mine would ever be.

Later that week, I talked to Riaz about his conversion. "How can you believe this stuff?" I blurted undiplomatically. "The beard, the toothbrush—all this trivia. How can it matter?"

It was late afternoon, and we were walking back and forth in the parking lot behind my mother's apartment building. He pondered my questions for a while, then said pensively, "Do you remember a conversation we had in Portland one rainy day, when you told me your philosophy of life? When you said your aim was to cultivate a stance of irony vis-à-vis everything?"

"Yes," I said. "It still is. No matter how sure you are, you might be wrong. That's what I mean by irony. It's the only stance that gives you room to reconsider. Without it, how can you know when you're going wrong? You have nowhere to stand except what you've chosen."

He heard me out patiently. Then he said, "Well, you asked that day what my foundation was. I had never thought about it in those terms, but I think my answer would center around earnestness. That's why I homed in on Islam. When I got to Pakistan, that's the first thing I noticed about the people—that quality of earnestness. And to me, from here and now, an earnestness based on faith is preferable to murky speculation."

"Okay, but your faith is too earnest. Your lifestyle is so austere. How many people are going to live like that? If this is what God demands, most of humanity is going to be excluded. How can that possibly be right?"

"I don't see it that way. To me, Islam points out a middle path between self-denial to the point of abuse and self-indulgent chasing after glitter and ostentation. Accepting Islam doesn't mean forsaking the world; it just changes the focus. The acts of living take on a meaning of which they are bereft in a materialist framework. Besides," he concluded simply, "I realized that Islam would work."

"Work for what? What do you mean 'work'?"

"If everyone followed these practices, none of today's problems would exist. Families would be rock-solid." He glanced at me. "There would be no warfare, no injustice, no division between the rich and the poor. No one would live in ways that despoil the Earth. People would devote themselves to other people instead of to things.

"Think about dating," he went on quietly. "You go to a movie with a girl. You sit side by side, looking at a screen. You're not relating to each other, but when it's over, you feel you've gotten closer in some way, even though you haven't even looked at each other for two hours, because you've been looking out together at the same thing. That kind of closeness comes about for Muslims when we say our prayers, except that what we focus on together is not a car chase or a murder, but God."

We went indoors then, and he gave me a present from Pakistan, a little Koran, cardboard cover, yellow pages, clumsy calligraphy, a peasant's Koran, but the Koran nonetheless. I felt oddly nervous taking it in my hands. I had feelings, I discovered, for the physical Koran that I had toward no other object. I worried about dropping it or doing it some irreverence.

That evening, I got an idea about how to approach my trip. Instead of telling people I was a writer looking for a story, I would tell them I was a lapsed Muslim looking for his roots. That might get people to open up more. I would learn a few verses from Riaz's Koran, so as to put the story across more effectively. But the very thought of using the sacred text in this calculated way triggered a twinge of dread. I didn't believe in a personal God, and yet I worried that my disbelief might make Him angry.

As I mulled it over, I had the Koran open before me, and my eyes were trying to puzzle out the first word of the first verse—not easy! But then I got it—and then something odd happened: The whole verse flared up inside me. I hadn't recited it in twenty years, yet I knew it like a times table. In fact, I found, the first ten verses of the Koran, the ones I had memorized in school, lived inside me, unforgotten.

I went to tell Riaz the news, but he was watching bigger news. The TV anchorman was reporting that the Soviet Union had poured 100,000 troops into Afghanistan. Wow, I thought. This can't be good. And it wasn't my trip I was worrying about this time; it was my father.

TANGIER

B Y THE TIME I LEFT the United States, I was already
down to $2,300. I had planned to linger in parts of
Europe, but I changed my mind once I got there
and just hurried from Paris to Madrid to Algeciras, hardly
stopping to sleep, or even to eat, because I could see that
European restaurants and hotels would drain the money
out of me like yogurt out of a cheesecloth bag. I figured I
could rest once I got to the Third World, the realm of
cheap. And I thought I was there at last when the ferry
from Algeciras docked at Tangier. As I disembarked, a
crowd of young men came swarming up the gangplank,
clamoring, "You want guide? Very cheap! Ten dirham. Five
dirham! Where you want go?"

Proudly, I told them I didn't need a guide; I was here to
learn about Islam. They acted impressed, but only so they
could stick to me as I made my way toward the Casbah.

The Casbah, as you may know, just means "the city," but it refers to the old part of town, the part built in Ottoman times. Every city in North Africa has a Casbah (sometimes called the Medina), and in 1980, every Casbah was a warren of winding alleyways too narrow for cars. I pushed my way through the crowds, trailed by a pack of volunteer guides. Every time I turned a corner, they shouted, "Not that way!" Every time I paused in front of a hotel, they shouted, "I know better one!" Wherever they said not to turn, I turned; in this way, I made my way to a hotel that looked decent.

After two sleepless days and nights on planes and trains, I needed to sleep, but I was too excited to stay indoors. No sooner had I stashed my bags than I went out to explore the streets.

Dust and dusk hung in the air outside—it was always twilight in the Casbah. Clusters of young men like the ones who had followed me from the docks lounged near my hotel. They had the stoned languor of hippies, and their broken English featured fragments of counterculture argot: "I dig it, man. Cool! Take it easy. Kick back." They even wore scavenged items of hippie clothing—this one wore boots, that one a leather vest; others blue jeans or T-shirts with American slogans on them. *Don't knock knockers: They've got you outnumbered 2 to 1. Make love, not war.* They asked where I was from, and when I said the United States, they cheerfully mimed shooting pistols and said, "Bang bang! Cowboys!"

"That's Texas," I corrected them. "I come from a city called San Francisco."

They brightened at this name and mimed shooting pistols at me. "Bang bang! Karl Malden! *The Streets of San Francisco*. What do you want to see in Tangier, my friend? I will guide you. Best bazaars. Very cheap. What you want to buy?"

"Nothing," I said, "I'm here to learn about Islam."

"One God, not two," a young man piped up helpfully.

"And Muhammad," another recollected, "was His messenger."

"I know that. I grew up in Afghanistan—"

"Afghanistan!" They cried, all excited now. They mimed shooting pistols at me. "Russians! Bang bang! Muslims support Afghanistan!"

I couldn't get away from them. I had to retreat back to the hotel. But when I came out later in the evening, they were still there, lurking in doorways up and down the block. Lounging on the street and emitting mellow vibes was part of their job description. These guys were working. Each motion of mine set up a corresponding motion among them. As I emerged from the hotel, they emerged from their shadows, ambling nonchalantly on a vector calculated to intercept my path as if by happenstance, so as to fall in beside me and commence their mellow-dude routine. I soon learned what other travelers must have learned: that I had to hire one of them to keep the rest at bay. I chose a wiry fellow about my age called Mohammed.

He wore boots with high heels that clicked on the cobblestones of the narrow streets. His T-shirt read *U.S.S. Texas—Bullship of the Fleet.* I got to know him a little over the days. His family lived in a village in the Atlas Mountains. He spoke with feeling about his mother's couscous, his boyhood friends and their games, his family's farm up there, reminding me of my own ancestral village of Deh Yahya, near Kabul. Did he go home to his village often? I wondered. "Yes. Every year, once, twice." Was it far? "No, not far." Why not go more often, then? He shrugged. "I must stay in Tangier now. I am businessman." Oh? What business? "I help tourists." On a typical day, I learned, he started working at eight or nine in the morning. He went to the docks to meet the ships from Algeciras and Málaga. When he spotted young people with backpacks, especially blond ones, he zeroed in.

Mohammed spoke a crude but serviceable Rube Goldberg brand of English, and a pidgin French and German, too. Tangier was, after all, an "international tourist center." And he knew what the tourists wanted. In the afternoons, on the rue des Postes, which led to the black market of Tangier, he competed with fifty other "businessmen," giving tours of the Old City. When the tour was over, the business began. "You want, I can get hashish, you—little bit: ten, twenty grams. You smoke in the hotel. Some guy, he make big deal, he fight you. Me, I only want to make some friend, relax you. No problem."

It was strange. The Americans whom I considered "my" people—counterculture folks who traveled east on the

Marrakech Express looking for "real life"—had created characters like Mohammed. In the rich part of town, free-spending jet-setters had spawned high-rise luxury hotels with Berber waiters in gold-braided suits; here in the poor quarters, Western hippies had turned working-class tough guys into simulacrums of hippies who weren't really hippies, but they didn't really fit into Moroccan society, either. And those same hippies returned to America convinced (although wrongly, I believe) that they had become a touch Moroccan.

And these tough guys were not really as tough as I thought them to be. Mohammed treasured a letter he had received five or six years ago from one of his customers: an American girl. He had it in his pants pocket, and when he took it out to show me, he had to unfold it carefully because it was tattered from much handling—the folds were almost worn through. It read, in full: "I hope you and your family are all well. You must work on your English, Mohammed." He had been reading this note over and over for years.

I stayed in Tangier a little over a week. Usually, I dismissed Mohammed as soon as I got into the old city; I paid him his full four-dollar daily fee. He was then free to find other customers on the rue des Postes, and I was free to roam the Casbah. The narrow alleys, the three-story houses closed to the public, all front, no seam: Yes, I was certainly in the Islamic world now. The alleys reminded me of Kabul's Shari-kuhna, "the Old City," where Uncle Ghani lived, but the complex mixture of odors, sweat and sewage and must, now struck me as repulsive. I felt ashamed of my reaction.

I stopped to chat with everyone who seemed willing, offering my carefully rehearsed cover story as a conversation starter—the one about having been born and raised a Muslim in Afghanistan, having spent many years in the United States, being on a quest now to see what the religion of my childhood might have to offer me. It was like wandering into a convention of Jehovah's Witnesses and saying, "I'm interested in changing religions; want to talk?" Yes, they did: Everyone did.

And I got the cover story out with less compunction than I had feared, because it was so close to the truth. So close that I felt my psyche leaning out of myself to hear their answers—almost as if I had a personal interest in this issue and not merely a journalist's curiosity.

Back at my hotel each night, after pouring out a letter to Debby, I jotted notes from my day's interviews, but I never found much to jot. I kept prodding people to tell me about their childhood ambitions, their current prospects, their dreams, thinking this might lead them to the issues I had discussed with Franz Schurmann of PNS—poverty, injustice, suffering, colonial exploitation.

But no one would go there. All I heard was "God is one. He doesn't want people to drink alcohol. Pork is forbidden. If you steal, your hand must be cut off. Don't ever commit adultery. Shall I teach you how to pray? Women must not display themselves to strangers. Oh, I almost forgot: Get ready for the Day of Judgment."

Practically everyone I talked to had been a lax Muslim in the past but was trying to be a better one now.

Everyone hated the Moroccan king, but when I asked why, they said, "Because he is an atheist."

"How can you tell?"

"He drinks alcohol. He chases women. He dresses like a European."

I asked about Muammar Qaddafi, the Libyan strongman who was making a particular ass of himself on the world stage just then. "Is he a good Muslim?"

"No. Qaddafi is a Jew."

"A *Jew*? Really?"

"Oh yes," came the sage reply, "placed in power many years ago by the Israelis to blacken the reputation of Islam! How else can you explain his actions?"

"What about the Iranian leader? Khomeini?"

This tended to lock people up for a moment, the way contradictory commands lock up a computer. "Well . . . Khomeini is Shiite. . . ." Shiism and Sunnism are the two main branches of Islam, as I mentioned earlier, and Moroccans are Sunnis. It reminded me of a talk show I'd heard once in America, about whether Catholics could be considered Christians. Generally, the Moroccans came around to allowing that Khomeini was a Muslim, and once they got that far, they were able to work up some enthusiasm: "He is *sincere;* he is even a mujahid, a warrior for the cause of Islam. The Iranians and the Afghans—they are the front line now, in the battle for the honor of Islam."

"But on opposite sides, of course."

"Opposite? No! They are brothers, arm in arm."

"But Iran is battling the United States. The Afghans are battling the Soviet Communists. Those are opposite sides."

"Soviets, Americans—same thing."

A few times in Tangier, some stranger reacted to my cover story by hauling me off to a room hidden away from the crowded bazaar to meet a "real Muslim." The most extreme case was Abdullah. I'll let that encounter stand for all of them. On my second day in Tangier, I heard about Abdullah from a group of men lounging in a vegetable store. He was a "true Muslim"; they could arrange a meeting with him, but I would have to come back.

When I went back, a secretive young man in a shabby suit said, "Come with me," and plunged into the Casbah without looking back. His secrecy puzzled me, but I followed him. We came to a covered alleyway, more shadowy than the rest of the Casbah; he told me to wait. He went through a nondescript doorway, then popped his head out and beckoned.

I entered a spare storefront that displayed a few small rugs, a few shoes, a cassette deck, a suitcase—in short, a motley collection of unrelated items. The place was crowded with men conducting what seemed to be a lively debate in Arabic, but the stocky shopkeeper dropped out of it to talk with me. This was Abdullah. He had a convict's crew cut and pug ears on a bullet-shaped head, but his small eyes twinkled with friendship, and his whole manner was bluff, sincere, and good-natured. He spoke decent English. "Which city you are from in America, mister? . . .

San Francisco? It's a beautiful city. I was there one time. I had fish on the Fisherman's Horf. Horf?"

"Wharf," I said. "Yes, that is a famous tourist spot."

He allowed a civil pause, then got down to business. "So. You want to become a Muslim?"

"Well"—he was coming on a little strong, I thought— "to learn about it anyway. . . ." I gave him my cover story.

"Excellent," he said. "That is the way it starts." He translated my story for the others, and they all looked pleased. Abdullah said, "Well, first, watch us pray and see how it is done. Then we can talk."

He led the way to the floor above the shop. A pious-looking white-bearded old man in a turban came up with us. We entered a well-swept room, bare of furniture, with white walls and a low, corrugated blue ceiling. Two small windows gave a cramped glimpse of the street below. Abdullah closed them and lit a stick of incense. His friend turned out all but one dim light. I felt an odd sense of déjà vu, for my college friends and I used to take these very same steps in preparation for smoking marijuana.

Abdullah's friend then spread a large light brown mottled animal-skin rug on the floor. A mat was placed at the foot of the skin for me. Both men pulled long white gowns over their street clothes.

"We wear these special clothes to pray," the shopkeeper explained. "This is sunna."

They stood side by side on the small mat and began their prayers. I was struck at once by how familiar the ritual seemed, like finding a light switch in the dark automatically in a house where you've once lived. But then I became aware of a spidery precision in their performance, a sharp contrast to prayers as my grandmother or my stepuncle, Dada Gul, had said them in old Afghanistan. I remembered them relaxing into prayer as a welcome break from the rigors of the day. For these guys, the prayer itself was a rigorous task that consumed energy. They wore absorbed expressions throughout, like scholars concentrating on a difficult text.

When they were through, we all went back downstairs. Abdullah gave me the usual instructions about the tenets of Islam, then added, "And a Muslim must advise. That's the most important."

"Advise?"

"Yes. He must advise his family, his friends, his brothers. If he sees them straying from the path, he must go to them and say, 'God has forbidden this; do you understand?' He must advise his brother to find the sunna of the Prophet."

"The sunna, you keep saying—is that different from the *sharia*?"

"Yes," he said. "The sunna is the way the Prophet lived his life. God gave us the sunna of the Prophet as an example. When Muslims follow the sunna, God helps the community. When we don't, God withdraws His favor, and the community becomes weak. Every misfortune comes upon it then, and people say it's bad luck, but it is not luck.

Everything is the will of the Almighty. For example, we don't pray in the mosque, because they don't follow the sunna. They call themselves Muslims, but they are careless and make many mistakes. God does not like this. You will find such carelessness all over the Muslim world. That is why the state of Muslims has fallen so low and why Europe has trampled on us all these centuries."

"What do they do wrong in the mosque?"

"When we pray, you notice, we hold out this finger at the time of bowing." He held up his hand with the little finger raised and the rest folded.

"I didn't notice."

"This finger! Like this! Weren't you watching?" He held his hand up again. "This means 'one God.' It is just a reminder, but it is the sunna, and you *must* do this. But in the mosque, they don't. When you pray, you're supposed to recite the *fatiha,* then one of the shorter suras, but between the *fatiha* and the sura, you are supposed to pause a few seconds. Do they pause in the mosque? No, they rush directly from *fatiha* to sura." Suddenly, he yielded to passion. *"This is not sunna!"* he thundered. Then he mastered his agitation and continued expounding on the mistakes of the mosques.

I could not easily follow his discourse, because every four or five sentences, some of the other men would break in to argue a point. "In the mosque," Abdullah told me, "when they fold their hands across their bellies, they rest the thumb here—above the navel! But this is not sunna! The thumb must be below the navel—"

"No! Not below it—on it!" A black-bearded, thick-lipped young man broke in, setting off a long argument in voluble Arabic, complete with plunging arms and pointing fingers. I was astounded that men who placed such great emphasis on the exact details of the rituals could disagree on so many points. Finally Abdullah declared, "So you see? This is why we don't pray in the mosque. Their prayers have no benefit, because they have forgotten the sunna. Do you know why they have forgotten it?"

I shook my head.

"Because the religious scholars have sold themselves to the governments."

"And the governments benefit, somehow, if people practice Islam incorrectly?"

"Of course. When the people are lost, the gangsters are safe. The governments want people to forget Islam entirely!"

"You don't consider the government of Morocco to be Muslim?"

"Ha-ha! Muslim? They are Mafia! Just like in Iraq! Saudi Arabia! Egypt! Gangsters! Zionists! Prophet Muhammad, peace be upon him, said, 'If there's enough for one, there's enough for two.' Do you think in a Muslim government that the people would be sleeping in the streets and the officials would be driving deluxe American automobiles?"

"In the West, people picture a Muslim as a fat rich guy lolling on cushions."

"Those gangsters in Saudi Arabia," he said bitterly. "That's why they pay the religious scholars to sow confusion. When the people's own ways don't shine, they follow European ways. Algeria follows France, Libya follows Russia, Egypt follows America—everywhere today, European ways rule Muslim lands. In Morocco, the king and his ministers wear *jullabas* in public, but when the doors are closed, the alcohol comes out, the women parade in miniskirts and less, and the men sleep indiscriminately with one another's wives. Even among ordinary people, my friend, you can see this happening. Girls in miniskirts up to here—" He indicated a spot far up his thigh and then shouted, "Look! There go two of them now!" He pointed indignantly through the window.

I looked, but what I saw were two girls in long-sleeved dresses with hems down to their calves and scarves over their heads. "They might as well be wearing lipstick in *both* places!" Abdullah fumed.

How could we be seeing two such different things? Which of us was crazy? What, I wondered, would Riaz have seen?

The thick-lipped young man thrust a photograph at me. It showed him and Abdullah flanking a frail old man with a very long snowy beard. "This Zamzama," he told me eagerly. "He great Muslim of Morocco."

"Is he a member of the ulama?" I asked. The ulama are the traditional religious scholars whose opinions rule the doctrine of Islam.

"No!" the young man exclaimed. "Ulama hate this Zam-zama! Government afraid this Zamzama, because he speak only truth, always truth."

"He is a great Muslim," Abdullah agreed. "Four years ago, I used to drink wine, ignore the sunna. Zamzama advised me. Now God is helping me to become better Muslim. He will help you, too. Just start praying, and He will teach you."

In 1980, there was no such thing as the Internet, no e-mails, and no personal computers even. You couldn't direct-dial an international call. You couldn't place one at all from the street in places like Morocco. There was nothing but snail mail, as it's called now. Before I left the United States, I had given my itinerary to Debby, and she had promised to write to me every day. Whenever I reached a new city, she said, I could go to general delivery and pick up her letters. But my itinerary had changed in the field. I had passed through Europe too hurriedly to get to a post office. In Tangier, I visited the Poste Restante every day, and I fired off letters to Debby and my other friends, but I never got a letter back. Probably Debby's letters were piling up in Paris. But I had been sending her letters informing her of my new itinerary and, in case she had forgotten, of my passion for her. I figured I would get a letter from her in Tangier if I simply waited long enough.

It was hard, though. I didn't like Tangier. I was spending sixteen dollars a day just for a hotel room and a guide I wasn't using. I wondered if I should move on to Algeria and wait for Debby's letters in Oran.

I headed for the train station to check out fares and schedules. Mohammed was not around, so I tried to sneak through the gauntlet of tour guides—not a chance. One of them locked me into his sights, trailed me for a block, then picked up his pace. I picked up mine, but he kept gaining. To pull away, I would have to run, and I didn't want to.

Not that I was in any trouble. It was broad daylight and the streets were crowded. I slackened my pace, just to show him I was not afraid, and he came alongside of me, maintaining the professional pretense of being on a casual afternoon ramble, headed nowhere in particular. "Hello. You need guide, no problem."

"No!" I snapped angrily. My patience was exhausted. I was running out of money, and this guy wanted five bucks just to leave me alone. "No guide," I shouted.

"You need guide?" he said. "Hello, I help you, very good, no problem. I get you some very good hashish, no big deal. You smoke in your hotel, just relaxing, no hassle, man. Where are you from?"

"Leave me alone! I don't *want* a guide."

"Where are you going? I am going that way, too, no problem. You are from America? Texas! Cowboys! America, no hassle, man. You want hashish? Very mellow, if you want to smoke it in your hotel, big fuckin' deal, man."

"Look, I can't stop you from going my way, but you are not my guide, okay?"

"No problem, mister, I am mellow. Where you are from in America, what city?"

"San Francisco."

"*Streets of San Francisco!* No big deal. You want to know Morocco? I will show you real Morocco, not for fucking tourists. I show you the real Morocco; it's mellow, man. You like hashish?"

I sped up, but he did, too, allowing no dead air between us, continuing to emit his derivative hippie patter. He really had the gait down: Even at top speed, he managed to look like he was strolling aimlessly.

He didn't come into the train station with me, but when I hit the street again, he was still there, waiting to reattach himself. On a weed-choked field within sight of the lightless Casbah, I said to him, "Here we must part ways. I'm going to my hotel now. Good-bye."

He sucked in his lower lip and said, "Twenty dirham, no problem."

Bile rose in my throat. "I didn't hire you. You didn't guide me anywhere. You just followed me. I owe you nothing."

"Okay, fifteen dirham," he said humbly. "It is my lowest offer. All day I was with you; it is good price. I must have fifteen dirham."

"We're not bargaining. I told you to leave me alone, and you wouldn't. You should be paying me! I don't owe you anything—understand? Nothing."

His unctuous cheer slipped away, as did his air of humble entreaty. His eyes flashed. "You rich man, you are so hungry. So hungry man!"

The phrase snagged me. Someone else might have found the epithet obscure or comical, but I knew what he meant. We have the same idiom in Farsi. *Hungry* means "greedy"—and not just ordinary greed, but cruel and ravenous greed. I had to argue back.

"I am not rich. I am far from home. I am a traveler." Instinctively, I fell back on that language: In Afghanistan, the word *traveler* carries tremendous weight. It trumps "poor."

But that idiom, apparently, didn't translate to Moroccan hippie English. "Hungry man!" he cursed.

And now I heard a chorus of "Hungry man." I looked up—we had attracted some twenty of these snaggle-toothed stragglers. Up close in this unforgiving sunlight, their poverty showed starkly. Every one of them looked unhealthy. They all had bad or missing teeth. Their cast-off American hippie clothes all looked threadbare.

The guides were on his side, of course. To them, I had used up a man's afternoon and was now refusing to pay him. "Hungry man! Pay his money!" someone howled.

Others took up the chant. "Pay him, hungry man!"

Suddenly, in a move so weird, it freaked me out, the guy dropped to his knees and began running his fingers over my shoelaces. "I want your shoes," he said.

"What?"

"If you won't give me fifteen dirham, give me your shoes."

All courtesy had drained out of him. I wouldn't say he emanated menace, but he had stopped trying to charm me, and his need lay nakedly exposed. The growing crowd muttered, "Hungry man! Give him your shoes!"

Well, I made an executive decision at that point. Most of my money was hidden in a money belt under my shirt. I took out my wallet, extracted all the bills in there, about thirty dirham, and thrust them into his hand. "This is all I have. Take it." With a hiss, the whole crowd craned for a closer look.

He hesitated. A moment ago, this much money would have looked princely. Since then, however, he'd decided on my shoes. Now he faced an agonizing choice: money or shoes? Money or shoes? He chose money. Maybe I looked like I would fight him for the shoes.

"No problem," he muttered. "Big fucking deal, man. I am mellow."

I walked away immediately. After about twenty feet, I looked back and saw him sitting on the ground, one of his shoes off. Even from a distance, I could see that his thin nylon sock had a hole where his big toe protruded.

Back at my hotel, I packed up my stuff. It wasn't an ideal time to leave. Insomnia had woken me at six o'clock that morning, the day had been tense and tiring, and I always had trouble sleeping on trains, but suddenly, I just wanted to be out of Tangier by nightfall.

CROSSING MOROCCO

O N   T H E   T R A I N   A C R O S S   M O R O C C O ,   I tried to hammer out a story for PNS on my tiny portable typewriter, but I didn't get far. It felt dishonest. It felt like the story I could have written without leaving home. I was using the quotes I had gathered to prove what Franz Schurmann and I had already decided was true: that people had turned to Islam out of poverty and desperation. But who were we to claim that all this rage and fervor wasn't really about tenets and beliefs, but about economics? Practically everyone who talked to me about Islam fixated on alcohol, short skirts, the *sharia,* and believing in one God. I was just refusing to take them at their word. I remembered my brother contrasting Islam to the "materialist framework." Actions in the materialist framework, he had said, were bereft of meaning. Was I not merely trying to recast the whole situation in materialist terms? Wasn't I saying, in essence, that Islamic revolutionaries talk religion but really just want more material goods?

And wasn't that exactly what a materialist *would* say? Perhaps I was describing myself, not them.

What if the revolutionaries really were fueled by spiritual and not material hunger? I was reminded of Nadi Ali, a model town near Lashkargah, where we used to go every New Year's Day for a big fair that featured Pashtun tribal dancing. The government built Nadi Ali as a place to settle nomads. It was a tidy village full of stone bungalows, each with its own irrigated garden plot, running water, electricity, lights, heat, the works. There was no shortage of nomads to settle there, for they were always passing through the area in caravans of fifty to seventy-five people, with their camels, their fat-tailed sheep, their dogs, their tents. They didn't own much else. When they got here, they had just crossed some of the world's harshest desert and now were on their way over mountain passes sixteen thousand feet above sea level, through snow up to their asses—for what? To reach some remembered pasture and later maybe trade some nuggets of dried camel yogurt for mirrors and eye shadow so their young men could go a-courting next time they crossed paths with a band of distant cousins.

The government was offering these harshly impoverished nomads a life of comfort, with plenty to eat, warm clothing, medicine, security, and the opportunity to accumulate money and goods. The nomads, virtually without exception, rejected the offer. They wanted to live in tents, move every week, and live on whatever they could milk from their sheep and camels, never knowing what catastrophe might lie over the next ridge. They had to be forced to settle in Nadi Ali, and soldiers had to be posted around the ideal town to keep them from escaping their good fortune. They were rejecting money and goods—for a way of life. For distinct experiences of love and nature and belonging, for certain sacraments of death and marriage and birth. These are not goods, nor even just "ideas." They're nodes in webs of meaning—the thing of which, according to Riaz, the materialist framework is bereft.

I put my notebooks away and picked up a book. I had left America with a suitcase half-full of books about Islam and one work of fiction, *The Studs Lonigan Trilogy.* I read them on planes and trains and left them behind as I finished them. The trilogy was somewhere in France. Now on the train across Morocco, I was reading an intellectual history of Islam by an erudite Pakistani scholar named Fazlur Rahman. His account of one doctrinal dispute in the early centuries of Islam hooked me. I couldn't stop thinking about it, couldn't stop spinning out the implications—and I have been thinking about it ever since.

The dispute raged between orthodox scholars and a school called the Mu'tazilites, the "Rationalists." The two schools didn't disagree on how people should behave or what they should believe. Their debate centered on one of those questions so abstruse, they give scholars a bad name—namely, Are certain beliefs and behaviors good because God commands them? Or does God command them because they are good?

Hairsplitting, you say? Not so fast. If certain beliefs and behaviors are good only because God commands them, it means that God might change His directives at any time. Logically, it's possible that justice and charity would suddenly be foul and murder good. Incest and child molestation might be celebrated deeds, to which the best and most heroic of us aspire, while the moral and ethical weaklings among us would succumb to such corrupt and contemptible temptations as love, generosity, and hope.

Unthinkable, you say, that God would ever promulgate such an ethos? Why not—because it wouldn't be right? If you think that way, you've slipped over to the other side. You've assumed that right and wrong, good and bad have a status prior to God and more fundamental than He. If God cannot, from His own almighty and unknowable will, enjoin murder and cruelty as virtues, God is not limitless or omnipotent.

Unwilling to go there, the Mu'tazilites argued that the good was as fixed and absolute as God Himself. God's commandment therefore embodied principles that reason could discover. And those deep principles could be applied to all new situations. In short, they took the position that things change, but the good is eternal, and the Koranic compass allows one to keep finding true north amid the turmoil of history.

Their opponents thought God was the only absolute, the only fundamental, pure, uncircumscribable will. He could, in His omnipotence, determine freely what was good. A human, therefore, couldn't reason from God's explicit commands to original ideas, because that would be assuming that God's will was bound by what the human mind could conceive. They took the position that the Koran gave the prescription for freezing history. Until further word from God, things *shouldn't* change—and further revelations from God were not to be expected, because Muhammad had declared himself the Seal of the Prophets.

Significantly, this debate unfolded in a political context. Everywhere from Cairo to Delhi was Muslim at that point. Throughout the realm, a smattering of Arabs presided over oceans of locals. Everyone in the realm accepted Islam, however, so power ultimately resided in the religious ideology.

If the orthodox school was right, the Arabs owned this ideology. The orthodox doctrine implied that questions about right and wrong, about jurisprudence, laws, and contracts, could be resolved only by recourse to the word of God as revealed in a particular time and place. Therefore, anyone who had actually been in that time and place had a leg up on knowing the truth. Those would be Arabs—Muhammad's people, with Mecca and Medina in their possession. And anyone who knew someone who had been there had the second derivative of a leg up. And so on.

By contrast, if the Mu'tazilites were correct, any Muslim anywhere, anytime, could discover from studying the Koran and the life of Muhammad the principles on which

God's commandments were built. Judgment and reason trumped authority and eyewitness testimony. In their ideological scheme, the Arabs had no particular advantage.

The orthodox scholars won. As a result, the rational inquiry into the nature of good was dropped from the Muslim curriculum. From this time on, the principle intellectual activities of Islam centered on studying the scriptures and the history of the first Islamic community, because, according to the orthodox scholars, one had only to discover what God commanded and then obey His commandments to the letter.

If nothing could be found relating to a particular matter in all the scriptures, all the Prophet's sayings, and all the chronicled events of his life, one fell back on the consensus of Muhammad's community, meaning the conduct and traditions of his companions—Arabs to a man. In practice, this meant studying exactly how things worked in Mecca and Medina during Muhammad's lifetime and directly thereafter.

It struck me that if the Mu'tazilites had won, Islam might have developed along wholly different lines. The Mu'tazilite approach might have seen the Muslim revelations as a blueprint for dealing with historical realities— life is tough; people can be ruthless; nothing is permanent except change. Being good in a monastery is easy, but Muhammad didn't seclude himself in some monastery; rather, he waded into life the way we actually encounter it. He led a political community; he was a husband, a father, and a friend. He went into battle, dealt with prisoners, settled family quarrels, thwarted conspiracies, rooted out as-sassination plots, punished criminals, and concerned him-self with business matters. How do you deal with stuff like that and keep your hands clean? How do you reconcile the messy realities of history with the demands of the ethical life? Isn't that where the pressure plate meets the clutch in matters of spirituality? Could Gandhi have dealt with Hitler? Not clear. Could Muhammad? Much more probable.

The defeat of the Mu'tazilites translated to a temporary victory for the Arabs, but it also planted a conservative im-pulse in Islam that endures to this day. Jews put the com-ing of the Messiah in the future. Christians seek individual salvation by accepting Jesus as a personal savior. Islam, however, focuses on the first Muslim community as the core religious fact. It proclaims that the truth about human history was incarnated in a historical moment, from which we've been receding ever since. Throughout the centuries, therefore, renewal movements in Islam have tended to look backward, have tended to preach the doctrine of get-ting back to the way it was.

Yet, if Rahman is right, fundamentalists are not actually going back to the beginning. They're going back to the outcome of a doctrinal dispute a century and more after the Hegira.

On my way across Morocco, I shared my compartment with six or seven other passengers. Whenever I wasn't reading, I was taking part in conversations, since most of my fellow travelers spoke French. One young fellow spoke only Arabic, however, and he stared at me with an interest that made me uncomfortable. It crossed my mind that he might be gay.

Nine or ten hours after I left Tangier, deep in the heart of Morocco, in the middle of the night, I had to switch trains. The interested young man got off, too. The station was deserted, and the connecting train wasn't due for hours. The young fellow tried to tell me something in pidgin French. *"Ici, nous, montre . . ."* It sounded like he wanted to show me something.

I didn't fully fancy leaving the station with this stranger, but then again, was I or was I not a macho journalist, hot on the trail of a big story? If yes, then shouldn't I jump at a chance to converse with a real Muslim in the real Morocco? So I nodded yes. My new friend led me to the street, and a car pulled up. A Moroccan was driving. My friend climbed in beside him. I was urged into the back seat, and we took off.

The town looked small on the map, but we drove for almost an hour through dark residential neighborhoods. At last, we came to a squat building with some lighted windows. The driver parked and we all got out. After a furtive look around, my friends led me down to a semibasement room, where I found a Berkeley coffeehouse, copied giant-size. The ceiling was low, but the walls, painted black, were so far away, I could hardly see them. The round coffeehouse tables seemed to extend forever, and music swelled from countless speakers affixed to the black ceiling: an old Hendrix record, followed by Cream, Led Zeppelin, B.B. King, and the like. A Moroccan man with kohl-rimmed eyes, dark irises, and pinpoint pupils served us thick, muddy-tasting coffee with lots of sediment. My two Moroccan friends watched for my reaction, hoping they had impressed me with the music and ambience, but nothing could have impressed me (except for the stunned and sleepy thought, So much for the real Morocco), because I was beginning my twentieth hour without sleep and I just wanted to crash.

Around 4 a.m., the Moroccans took me back to the station and I boarded a train for the Algerian border. I was too jazzed on Moroccan coffee to doze, so by the time I arrived in Oujda, the town nearest the border, I had not slept a wink in twenty-eight hours.

As I stumbled off the train, a middle-aged man moved in on me. I instantly recognized a member of the Fraternal Order of Moroccan Tour Guides. His hand raked at my sleeve. "You want I change money for you? Better than banks."

"I just want to find the bus to Algeria."

"I take you to bus station, no problem. Very cheap. Free. Because you famous personality. You want how much Algerian dinar? I give you six hundred dinars for one hundred dollars. Banks exchange you three hundred for one hundred. Six hundred is better. Three hundred bad, no?"

I was too tired to say no. And six hundred did sound better than three hundred. I was planning to stay in Algeria for a few weeks at least—I could use a good chunk of Algerian money. And for once, I did need a guide, for I had no idea where the bus station was. So I yielded to this man.

Next thing I knew, he was tugging me into a bank. He couldn't take a traveler's check, you see. He needed me to cash a traveler's check for a hundred dollars and then give him those dollars in exchange for dinars.

But the bank had never heard of American Express. The teller said, "Is that all you have?"

"It's American Express!" I bleated.

"You don't have National Bank of Morocco?"

"No. Just American Express, but—"

"Thomas Cook?"

He went through ten or twelve other types of traveler's checks he would accept, each one more absurdly obscure—Liverpool Municipal Bank, International Farmer's Credit Union, Leeds Haberdashery and Insurance. The only financial institution on earth he'd never heard of was American Express.

Three or four stops later, we found a bank willing to take a chance on that fly-by-night, little-known institution, American Express. I stood at the counter, reeling with fatigue as I signed my name. I rushed out, gave the guy a hundred dollars, and got a thick wad of Algerian bills. Only then did he finally consent to take me to the bus station, where I'd board a bus for the Algerian border. I felt so grateful to be leaving Morocco.

THE BORDER

T HE MOROCCAN BUS went only to the border, not across it, because there was bad blood between Morocco and Algeria. You had to walk across a no-man's-land of thirty or forty feet, check in on the Algerian side, and there board an Algerian bus for Oran.

The Algerian guards spoke no English, but they scanned my passport and waved me to a shed for processing. There, while sitting on a bench, awaiting my turn, I saw the big sign on the opposite wall: IT IS FORBIDDEN TO BRING ALGERIAN MONEY INTO ALGERIA.

I gulped and went outside to think. Should I tell the authorities about my six hundred illegal Algerian dinars? Would they confiscate the money? I could not afford to give up a hundred dollars! Quietly, I transferred the roll of Algerian money from my hip pocket to my inside jacket pocket—and there touched something that scared the hell out of me: only one packet of traveler's checks instead of two. I emptied my pocket and my eyes confirmed what my fingers had discovered. I had lost my sealed packet of traveler's checks: thirteen hundred dollars. Just like that, I was down to my last eight hundred.

I must have left those checks at the bank in Oujda, I thought. I rushed back to the border, but the guards blocked my way. "No one is allowed to enter Morocco from Algeria."

"No, no, you don't understand. I never really left Morocco. I was just—"

The guard pointed at my feet. "You are standing on Algerian soil now. No one is allowed to come into Morocco from . . . there."

"But I have to go back. I left my money in Morocco."

"Your money is in God's hands now."

Well, American Express had an office in Algiers, so my only hope now was to get to Algiers as fast as possible. Maybe I could get my money refunded. I went back to the Algerian processing shed. The official stamped my passport and said, "How much money are you bringing in?"

"About eight hundred dollars in traveler's checks," I responded miserably.

"Have you got any Algerian money?"

I laughed nervously. "Where would I get Algerian money?"

He laughed, too, as if to say, It's my job to ask. Then he pointed at my suitcase. "What is in there?"

"Just personal stuff."

"Show me." He opened my bag, and his attention

moved to the packet containing some photos of Debby that I had shot on the beach at Point Reyes a week or two before I left California. "What's that?"

"Photographs."

"Pornography?" He frowned.

"No!" I searched for a word and settled on the one I would have used with Afghans. "My fiancée!"

He opened the packet and flipped through the pictures, then slammed the suitcase shut. "Your fiancée is very beautiful. Now you must cash one hundred dollars of your traveler's checks."

"Cash a check?"

"Yes. To enter Algeria, you must buy at least one hundred dollars' worth of Algerian dinars."

I already had a hundred dollars' worth of Algerian dinars, but of course I couldn't tell him that. I took another tack. "When I leave, I can change back whatever I haven't spent?"

He smiled at my naïveté. "No. You must spend at least one hundred dollars in Algeria."

Or two hundred, as the case might be. Well, I'd have to absorb the extra dinars into my expenses somehow. No one would ever know.

I signed over another of my precious checks. The official gave me three hundred dinars and handed me a form. "Each time you spend money or cash a check in Algeria, it will be recorded here. When you leave, the amount you have spent must equal the amount you have cashed, plus the amount you still possess. Understand?"

CROSSING ALGERIA

AFTER THE HECTIC CORRUPTION of Morocco, Algeria felt wonderfully spare and orderly. I was in a socialist country now, thank God. No assaultive guides, no bickering and bartering, no Mercedes-Benzes plowing through crowds of beggars. I tried to savor it, but I couldn't. My wallet was half-empty. My stomach was all clenched. For me, the bus to Oran could not go fast enough.

The men on the bus—there were no women—struck up easy conversations with me. I told my story, and they started talking. Everyone wanted to make friends.

There was another American on the bus, too. To my eyes, his unshaven chin, his shitkicker boots, his hip-hugging Levi's, and his bandanna said *tough mother-fucker*. In some biker bar in north Portland, he might well have intimidated me. Here in Algeria, surrounded by

Arabs, he didn't look so tough. The Arabs attached no meaning to his clothes and hair. He might just as well have been wearing Bermuda shorts. Power is a social construct, right down to the kick-ass level.

We struck up a conversation. His name was Jake. He was on his way to Libya to work for an American oil company.

But when I got off at Oran, so did he. Three of the Algerians from the bus showed me the way to the post office, and Jake came along. The post office had no letters for me. The Arab guys offered to take me to a good restaurant, and Jake fell in with us without asking. I told him I wasn't going to stay in Oran that night; I was going to push on to Algiers because I was anxious about my traveler's checks. This time, I told him, I was going to get a sleeping car. Jake said, "Yeah, we'd better keep going," as if we were partners.

At the restaurant, a small local place, with nary a tourist in sight, I picked up the tab since, what the hell, I was flush, right? When the check came, however, the waiter asked for my financial form. He stamped it and wrote the cost of the meal in the allotted space. Even in this local joint, the state was watching. Suddenly, the roll of black-market dinars in my pocket felt huge. I told Jake my dilemma, but he only advised me, "Keep it hidden, man."

We took a cab to the train station (and the cabdriver recorded the cost on my form). At the ticket booth, I asked for a first-class ticket to Algiers in a sleeper, and—oh well—one for Jake, too. The man mumbled a price, took our money, and stamped our forms, but all he gave me were two scraps of paper with numbers on them. I said, "What's this? This doesn't look like a first-class ticket. I need a sleeping car tonight. It's very important." I was now entering my thirty-eighth hour without sleep.

The ticket agent smiled at my naïveté. "Here you buy a general ticket. On the train, you talk to the conductor and upgrade to first class."

It sounded like some kind of bribe system to me. The real price of this sleeping car would emerge only after negotiation. Oh well, at least a bribe would not be stamped on my financial form.

In my sleep-deprived state, voices and sounds had taken on that random volume thing and lights all had halos, as in a mist, only there was no mist. Once in a while, my ability to focus broke and I felt surrounded by a chaotic, rumbling, eruptive, intense simultaneity of noise and event. I could function just barely well enough to go along with whatever program I was handed, so I accepted the nondescript ticket.

With his ticket paid for, Jake was now my sidekick. Whatever I said sounded good to him.

My sidekick, but not my helper. I'd gotten the cab. I'd ordered the food. I'd found the train station. I'd bought the tickets and established the situation with the ticket seller. Well, Jake couldn't be blamed, I thought. After all, he didn't speak French.

Across the street, I glimpsed several French-language newspapers on display. Even from a distance, the headlines telegraphed alarming international news, although it wasn't exactly news to me. I had been catching snippets and snatches of the worsening scene all the way from Tangier.

Soviet tanks were crushing Afghanistan. Blood was running in the streets of Kabul.

The Iranian "students" occupying the American embassy were making bombastic threats and there were rumors of torture.

American tourists had been stoned in Syria.

American diplomats had been attacked in Egypt, much to the chagrin of Egyptian government officials, who were so resolutely pro-American. Egypt had been censured by the Arab League, which was calling for an Arab boycott of all things Egyptian. Libya had vowed to close its border with Egypt and not to let so much as a rat cross in either direction.

The American embassy in Libya had been burned down.

"How do you feel about Libya now, Jake?" I asked.

"Did they say anything about the oil companies?"

"No, just the embassy."

"Well, there you go, see. The oil companies, they're different. I'm not into politics, man."

"I don't think you have to be into politics to be in trouble in Libya."

"Well, I'm going, man. I got a job there."

"As an overseer of Arabs? Working for an American oil

company? In Libya? Today? Jake, maybe you should re-think your plan. It might be hard giving orders to a crew of Arab workers right now."

"They give you whips, I think."

"Whips?"

"Yeah, I'm not worried, man. They give the managers whips."

I was just wishing I could scrape this guy off me.

"And in the oil fields, they got guards," he went on. "The embassy dudes got all this diplomatic bullshit to deal with. They can't just shoot people. But the oil companies, man, some fuckers start giving them trouble, blam. I'm not worried."

"Ever whip anyone, Jake? Or shoot someone?"

"No, man. You?"

"No, and I don't think I could. How about you? Could you shoot someone?"

"Fuck yeah, man. I could shoot the fuckers. Self-defense, man."

"Except that you don't have to be there."

"What else'm I gonna do? I've come a long way, and I don't have the bread to get back. Pay's good, from what I hear."

In the United States, I would have put a great distance between me and this guy right away. Here in Algeria, he felt like my wayward brother: much in need of correction and advice, yes, but still our clothes, our language, even our most trivial shared cultural references—Superman, Eddie

Haskell, Wilt Chamberlain, Santa Claus, "Strike three," "Fries with that?"—bound us together. It was seven-thirty. The train was due to leave at eight. We made our way outside to wait. The platform was roped off, but a line had formed behind the rope, a hundred people or so. That's not many for a train, so I wasn't worried, just tired. I could see a big clock in a small shed where some railroad security men were drinking tea, ever so slowly marking off the minutes that stood between me and that sleeping compartment. I already knew this was going to be the best night's sleep I had ever enjoyed.

Jake, meanwhile, had been mulling over our conversation about Libya. "If it doesn't work out with the oil companies," he blurted, "think I'll head for South Africa."

"South Africa?"

"I hear a white man can get a job there, easy. And the pay's pretty good."

"I bet they give you a whip, too."

"Hell, man—they'd have to."

I shifted my weight to keep my legs awake. I could see the six policemen in their little building, sitting around a table, laughing sociably over their tea. They wore perfectly pressed gray uniforms with bits of red piping.

Out where we were standing, darkness had fallen. The line now stretched so far behind us that I could no longer see the end of it. I noted signs here and there, written in French, admonishing us to behave ourselves. SPITTING IN PUBLIC IS A DISGUSTING HABIT. ALGERIANS DO NOT

THROW GARBAGE IN THE STREET. PUSHING AHEAD OF OTHERS IN LINE IS RUDE. Each sign had a cartoon illustrating its point.

The big clock's hands inched toward the hour. A few moments before eight, the police turned their teacups over, pushed out their chairs, dusted off their jackets, marched out of their cabin, fanned out along the line, and began to club people. No provocation, no reason that I could see. I lifted my shocked gaze to the train.

A melee had broken out at the far end of the platform, people punching and clawing to get through the gate, trampling the few who had fallen to the ground and emitting a dull, caterwauling group roar. Now I understood why the policemen had finished their tea at a few seconds before departure time. Routinely at this hour, they had work to do. Quite without warning, the crowd erupted in my direction. I got knocked down just as the policemen burst through the line. I was clawing at the ground, moving like a crab to get out of the way, but not moving fast enough. A policeman came through the fallen ticket holders, clubbing to the right and to the left, back and forth. In nothing flat, he came to me, and his club descended. I parried the blow slightly, and it glanced off my head, but the next stroke caught me on the shoulder, a dull thud that left my arm feeling nerveless.

Then he was past me, and I was on my feet, running for the gate. I hadn't slept in thirty-eight hours, but pure adrenaline rendered me fully awake. Crashing off a fellow ticket holder, I found a path of least resistance—and suddenly found myself one molecule in a swift stream of human beings flowing smoothly through the ticket gate. The policemen were simply using their clubs to shape a rioting mass of ticket holders into a single file. That's all it was about. They looked bored.

I heard Jake behind me, panting and calling out. His eyes looked like broken eggs. He'd taken a hit or two. My eyes probably looked like his. My shoulder ached already, but at least I knew I was getting a sleeper—I didn't care about the cost. I was ready to spend my whole extra six hundred dinars for a good night's sleep.

Jake and I had been near the front of the line when all this started, but now we were bringing up the rear. I scrambled through the first open door. I just wanted to get on the train. Then I could find the conductor and upgrade to first class.

Every seat was filled. The aisles were jammed. Even the luggage racks above the seats were filled with people lying down, and others were yanking at them, trying to pull them down and take their places.

"*Le conducteur!*" I yelled. "*Où est le conducteur?*"

Eventually, a curious Algerian who had a seat and thus the leisure to attend to my question asked why I wanted to see the conductor.

"To upgrade my ticket," I cried. "I want to be in first class."

Laughter rippled through the car. I heard one man letting a comrade in on the joke: "He wants to 'upgrade' his ticket."

Someone explained to me: "There is no first class, second class here. You're in socialist Algeria, brother. There is only one class here, first class, and you are in it."

"It isn't like this every night," someone else explained. "People have been in Oran for the weekend; now they are going home."

I had no choice but to push forward, looking for somewhere, anywhere, to sit. Jake stuck to me like an extra limb. We got extruded out of this car onto the little platform between cars, which was open on both sides. Young soldiers were bulging toward us out of the next car. We had reached the end of the line.

Even the platform offered standing room only. Two dozen of us were crowded into a space about five feet by seven—myself, Jake, and twenty young Algerian soldiers.

The soldiers were excited. The whole Islamic world was in an uproar. Just that weekend, Libyans had burned down the American embassy. Muslims triumphant; Western dogs, go home. Muslim power hooray; Yankee nothing: We spit on you, and what are you going to do about it? Fuck with us, we'll take more of you hostage. Yeah. We'll cut the heads off your so-called diplomats—your fuckin' spies.

Such was the exuberance of the young men on that platform. And what luck for them: Here on this dark eight-hour night train ride to Algiers were two Americans.

The teasing began at once. They had no malice toward us; they were just guys feeling good about being a bunch of guys, Muslim guys. They didn't mean us any harm, no, but clearly they didn't care whether we lived or died, either.

"Hey, Americans," they said jokingly in French. "Who's on top now? Bang bang! Eh? You're dead, eh?"

It felt a lot like being on the streets of San Francisco after the 'Niners won their first Super Bowl, twenty-something-year-old males roaming the streets roaring, "WE'RE NUMBER ONE!" But this "we" was bigger and more intense. For three centuries, the West had slowly been forcing the Muslim world to its knees, and not even noticing—that was the worst of it. Now at last—*this year! this weekend!*—Islam had risen again.

"You Americans think you will get to Algiers?"

"What'd they say?" Jake asked me. He was pressed against the back of the compartment, his eyes dancing with hostility and fear.

I blurted to the young men, "I am a Muslim."

They roared with laughter. "If you are Muslim, repeat your *shahada*."

"*Ash-hadu al la illa-ha il-allah u Muhammad u rusool-illah*," I recited—which means "I testify that there is no God but God and Muhammad is His messenger."

The jeering died away to a murmur. One of the young men patted my head and said, "What about *this* one—is *he* Muslim?"

"What'd he say?" Jake demanded.

"He wants to know if you're a Muslim."

"Tell him it's none of his fucking beeswax." He was grinning, but his bravado looked to be thinning.

I pretended to translate his words. "He says he is traveling to find out about Islam; he's here to learn. He respects your country."

"Tell 'em they better not lay a hand on me, man. I'm an American. Tell 'em Americans kick Algerian ass, man."

"Jake," I counseled. "Don't be talking about kickin' ass just now."

"Do you eat pig meat?" one of the soldiers shouted. "We don't eat pig meat."

"Me neither."

"We are Muslims; we don't eat pig meat."

"I'm a Muslim, too!"

"But you lived in America! *They* eat pig meat."

"Yes, but—"

"Does *he* eat pig meat?" Fingers pointed at Jake.

"Maybe in the past, but—"

"Does he eat snake meat?"

"No, I don't think so—"

"Does he eat horse testicles!" There was a raucous boom of laughter. And then they were all chattering and shouting suggestions at once: "Cow lips? Pig nostrils! Excrement!" One soldier said to me, "Traveler, you have seen these places. Tell us: Do Americans eat excrement?"

"No, they most certainly—"

"Brothers, we risk becoming unclean riding in this compartment with one who eats pig excrement!"

"Throw them off the train. What's to prevent us!"

They were still laughing; it was still a joke. I had to keep it that way.

"You're not going to throw a Muslim off your train." I guffawed, as if I could hardly imagine something so ridiculous. "No, no—we are all brothers. If one leaves, we all must jump off the train."

"Not you," the soldier said. "Him!"

"What's he saying? I'll kick his ass, man! Tell him Americans invented spaceships; we've been to the *moon*, man. What've Algerians done? We invented *television*! The A-bomb—how many fuckin' A-bombs does Algeria have?"

"No, no," I insisted, clapping my Algerian friends on their shoulders. "He is not worth it—look how he's shivering! Let's keep him on the train with us as a spectacle, an amusement. Why throw him off? So much trouble!"

"It's too crowded. We need room. He's a big one—"

Oh, how mightily I joked with my new Muslim brothers on that endless night. How aggressively I discussed Islam with them! What a merry crew we were, riding through the night on that dark platform open on two sides, our laughter carrying for miles on the whistling wind; me into my fortieth hour without sleep, hallucinating from fatigue, eight hours to go, struggling to stay jovial. I had to keep pushing into their space to keep them from swelling into mine, ours. Every time my energy flagged, they began to encroach on me with questions that moved quickly from friendly curiosity to boisterous humor to aggressive hilarity, and then to physical humor, a bit of pushing, a few good-natured threats.

At last, in the wee hours, the soldiers' energies waned. Voices fell silent one by one, until only the clacking of the wheels remained. One man fell asleep standing up, jammed against a wall. I was wishing I could sleep, but my senses stayed coiled like springs.

Finally, blessedly, the train pulled into the city of Algiers. Jake and I pried ourselves loose from the others and disembarked. It was eight o'clock and starting to drizzle. I had been awake for fifty hours now.

Jake wanted to find a hotel room, but I wanted to look for the American Express office first. I told him to go ahead, but he didn't want to leave me—out of loyalty, he said. He offered to carry one of my bags. I agreed. We stopped at a café and had some bread and cheese. I looked up the American Express office in my handbook—*Alhamdulillah!* It was on this very street, just a few blocks away. Salvation!

We quickly found the address. But it wasn't the American Express office anymore. It was some kind of government agency. Inside, I asked, "Can anyone tell me where American Express has moved?"

"American Express closed its office in Algeria six months ago," a man said. "Perhaps there is one in Tunis."

The whole headlong ordeal from Oran to Algiers had been for nothing.

I told Jake my bad news. There was nothing left but to get a hotel room now and crash for weeks. Jake agreed. By this time, the drizzle had turned to sleet. We could see some hotel signs farther up the street, so we hoisted our gear and headed there.

But the first place we tried had no vacancies. The second place had no vacancies. The third place had no vacancies. Not one hotel within walking distance of the train station in any direction had a vacancy.

This was the lowest moment of the trip. The night train from Oran hadn't frightened me, because I was too geared up. The loss of thirteen hundred dollars had shocked me, but I had options and actions to consider. Here in Algiers, I hit a wall. Can one die from fatigue and sleep deprivation? I was going to die. I felt sure of it at that moment.

Then I focused on a sign across the street. Le Bureau de Tourisme d'Algiers. The Algerian Tourist Bureau! We stumbled into the one-room office. A man sat sleepily behind the counter. I said, "Please, can you tell me how to find a hotel room? We've been looking all morning."

"There are no hotel rooms in Algiers at this time," he responded, looking us over with idle curiosity.

"Not a single one?"

"Not a single one."

"How can you tell? This looks like a big city. How can you possibly know there is not one single vacancy *anywhere*?"

"I know, because our great socialist government has appropriated all the hotels in Algiers to solve the housing shortage. The working people of Algiers are living in the hotels now."

"Where are tourists supposed to stay?"

"Tourists?" He gave me a fishy stare. "There are no tourists in Algiers, my friend. Algeria does not have a tourist industry."

"Isn't this the Tourist Bureau?"

He thought about this anomaly a moment, then allowed that it was so.

"How can you have a Tourist Bureau if you have no tourists?"

He raised a cautionary finger. "Ah! No tourists today—but Algeria may very well have an important tourist industry in the future. Our alert socialist government is prepared for every possibility."

"But what is your current function—do you have no current duties?"

"Of course I have duties! In fact, I am a very busy man, so if you have nothing further—"

"But what are your current duties? What is the purpose of this bureau right now?"

"To give information."

"About what, if your country has no tourist industry? What information do you give? And to whom?"

"Well!" He puffed up, and his mustache bristled. "I have just given information to *you*. I have informed you that there are no hotel rooms available in Algiers."

"Then where are we supposed to stay?" I moaned. "I'm going to collapse if I don't get some sleep."

He stroked his mustache thoughtfully. "Buy a ticket to Tunis. Go to see the ruins of Carthage. That is what tourists do. You can sleep on the train."

With heavy hearts we returned to the train station and bought tickets to Tunis. But again, the train baffled our expectations, this time by offering such luxuries that I felt heaven could wait. We got a *couchette*, a sleeping car, which we shared with six other passengers. By day, the little room had two long seats that accommodated the eight of us sitting up. At night, four small cots dropped down from the wall on each side, so each of us got a bunk. When night finally came, I slept like a chunk of lead for ten hours, and when I woke up (even though my shoulder hurt like hell), I felt systemically restored.

The eight of us in that compartment got to be great friends. We played cards, chatted, visited the dining car together. That first day, it's true, I was literally hallucinating from lack of sleep, but I had lucid moments, too, and I can still recover patches of bright memory. I remember the shy clerk, the guy with acne scars, the swashbuckling merchant. I remember Moedjid and Hocine best of all.

Moedjid reminded me of a middle-aged elf in a natty little suit. He claimed to be a devout Muslim—though not a learned one, he hastened to assure me. "I only know the essentials." He had a way of punctuating his remarks by slapping his fist into his palm and saying, "Phweet!"—meaning "Just like that!" or "Gone!" or "Done!"

For example: "I'll hang around Tunis till my money's gone, then—phweet!"

Four years ago, he told me, he had not been a good Muslim. "I used to gamble. . . . I used to drink—phweet! Black and White! Black and White! Black and White!" He mimed knocking back shot after shot of whiskey. "But then I changed. Suddenly? Yes, but it had been building up. My family are all practicing Muslims. I have ten brothers and two sisters—most are practicing Islam. They don't say anything to me, but every night when I come home drunk, I see the sadness in their faces. And then one day, I realize everyone is going to die. Sooner or later, everyone has to face the Judgment. Suddenly, I have a change of heart . . . the whiskey bottle—phweet. The cards—phweet. Now in Algeria these days, you have many people who ignore Islam—many! My brother, for example—he chases women, he drinks—all day he is busy doing what he shouldn't. But then he goes to sleep. From the moment he shuts his eyes until he wakes up the next morning, he is a good Muslim. But after that—phweet!"

"Is there tension between those who practice and those who don't?" I asked.

"Tension? No. Each to his own. Now me, I do the essentials. Only the essentials. I am not perfect. I admit it. I don't drink—although I used to— Black and White! Black and White! Now—phweet! I read the Koran . . . a little every day. Not too much. I perform my prayers. . . . But if a woman goes by with bare legs, I look at her legs. It is forbidden, I know that, but I look. I'm not perfect."

Hocine worked as a clerk in some government bureaucracy. His skin had a European pallor that suggested bicultural genes. He wore oversized glasses and a leather jacket, a striped T-shirt, khaki pants—European clothes with a Western flair. All the others, by contrast, wore nondescript suits, except for the merchant, who was decked out in Moroccan robes.

In fact, Hocine was a Euroculture groupie. He plied me with questions about the West. How tall were the buildings? What were the TV shows about? Did I go on dates? What was that like? Was it hard to travel within my own country? What kinds of papers did I need? None at all? Ahhh! He wanted to hear about hamburgers, and picnics, and cruising singles bars, about getting a paper each morning that provided uncensored news from everywhere! Everything I said dazzled him. Classified ads, for example: Could you really run your finger down columns and columns of different jobs and pick whichever one suited you? I tried to tell him, "Pick, yes, but get, that's something else." He didn't comprehend.

Tunis apparently was much more Westernized than Algeria. Hocine had long fantasized about going there and had been working toward the trip for years—longer than I had been planning mine. For him, the work had consisted mostly of obtaining the requisite documents, which I had knocked off in a few weeks. Saving the money had not been so hard, because Algerian law didn't permit him to leave his country with much money anyway. Algeria did not want its citizens escaping, and this regulation served as a cost-efficient leash.

"So you're going to Tunis with how much?"

"A hundred dollars. Yes."

"What can you do in Tunis on a hundred dollars?"

"Just look around."

"At what?"

"At the life. The city. The people."

"And then what?"

"If I have enough money, I might . . . I might go to . . . France." He grinned, showing big teeth and pink gums. His shy grin said he knew his ambition was outsized foolishness: Hocine setting foot on French soil? Who was kidding whom?

The next morning, as we sped toward the Tunisian border, I remembered that bundle of six hundred dinars. I couldn't possibly absorb them into my travel expenses now. I went to the bathroom, but you know what? I just couldn't flush them down. They looked like play money, but I knew they were real: the materialist in me, I guess. Finally, I split the bundle in two and put one bundle in each of my socks, under the sole of the foot. In Tunisia, I would trade them for dollars on the black market and take the inevitable beating on the exchange, lose everything I had gained in Morocco and more, but *c'est la vie.*

At the border, the train clanked to a halt. We sat waiting as steam billowed past the windows. I started to get nervous. I asked Moedjid what was happening, and he shrugged. *"Les gendarmes,"* he said.

The police? What did they want?

He shrugged again. "Always on the border, there is something."

The door blew open forcefully and two men in those same red-piped uniforms I had seen at the train station in

Oran stepped into our compartment. They spoke to the Algerians in Arabic. I didn't dare ask what they had said. Jake demanded to know what this was about, but no one answered him.

"Fuckin' fascism, man," he muttered.

The gendarmes beckoned Hocine to stand and started patting him down. Yow. Was this routine? Did everyone leaving Algeria get searched? Thank God I had transferred my illegal money into my socks.

Hocine was told to sit down and remove his shoes.

I could feel the lumps of money under my arches. Hocine, his chin sunk onto his chest, unlaced his shoes slowly. Very reluctantly, he pulled off his right shoe, then his left. The gendarmes yanked off his socks, and bills spilled onto the floor. The gendarmes laughed and shook their fingers at him in a playful, scolding gesture, but the arrogance of power colored their laughter.

One gendarme yanked Hocine to his feet. The rest of us watched under a heavy mantle of shocked silence. Jake burst out, "Well, Ansary, I guess they're going to find your money, huh?"

I glared at him. Just past his face, I could see the acne-riddled clerk clutching himself, his lips fixed in a mirthless grin. Jake shut up, but his knee kept on bouncing.

Hocine was led from the car, and I never saw him again.

Next, the merchant was made to stand up. He, too, was patted down and made to take off his shoes, but in the middle of this search, the second gendarme came back and conferred with the first in a low voice. While they were talking, the merchant quietly put on the shoe he had taken off, as if the search of him was over; and when the gendarme turned back, he started on Moedjid, who came out clean of contraband.

Now it was my turn. Both gendarmes had now crowded into the compartment. One of them began to question me in French. Who was I? Where was I going? To Asia, I replied. "Traveling, eh?" he declared with triumphant amusement. *"Et qu'est-ce que c'est?"* He lifted my portable typewriter with two fingers and a thumb, suspending it delicately at arm's length as if exhibiting a satchel of illegal drugs.

"I'm a writer," I admitted humbly.

"Ah! What kind of writer?"

Something told me this was not the time for the "looking for my Muslim roots" story. "I'm a cultural writer. I'm interested in food."

"Food. You have been in Algeria investigating . . . food?"

"Here and elsewhere. I'm writing a book about the food of many countries."

"Tell me, Mr. Food Writer, what have you learned about Algerian food?"

"Couscous is good."

The gendarmes both grinned, pleased with my answer. They moved on to Jake. A cursory search turned up nothing. Finally, they departed. The train didn't move for a long time. No one spoke. I kept listening for a noise, a scream, some sign, but we didn't know why we weren't moving, and we knew we never would.

In Tunis, I proceeded immediately to the general delivery window at the central post office: no letter from Debby.

I went to the street where the black market money changers hung out. "Who wants to sell me some currency?"

"Me!" they all clamored. "What have you got?"

"Algerian dinars. I want dollars."

The money changers burst out laughing. "That's shit money, my friend! No one takes Algerian dinars outside of Algeria."

I tried to give the dinars to my Algerian friends, but they didn't want to sneak the money back across the border. (I still have a roll of Algerian money in a junk drawer somewhere.)

Next day, I went looking for the American Express office, but I don't have to tell you what I found. It had closed months ago. I could try the one in Cairo. Or the one in Paris.

Cairo? Or Paris? Not a tough choice. I went to a travel agent and bought a ticket for Paris. My journey back to the edge of Afghanistan was over.

Before I left, Moedjid came to me, looking very pleased with himself. "I just pinched a woman on the street," he said.

"You what? Pinched a woman? Isn't that considered a sin?"

"Yes. It's true. I committed a sin. Why should I compound the offense by trying to deny it? God likes it better when you own up to what you have done. I sinned all right. I pinched the woman right on her—" He patted his rump. "Here's how it happened. I was standing here; she was easily within reach . . . there! I stretched out my hand and—phweet! I squeezed. By the time she looked around, my hand was at my side again. 'Did you do that?' she shouted at me. 'Oh pardon, yes. Excuse me!' I told her. What's the use of lying about it? I sinned. That's all there is to it. Her derriere was formidable!"

"I'm surprised at you," I said severely. "You probably made that woman very uncomfortable."

"Yes, I know. It was wrong." His voice grew subdued. "A friend of mine is even worse. When he sees unclothed women walking about, like this one I pinched, he all but loses control of himself. He can't keep his hands off them. He starts pawing at their legs, at their breasts. . . . It's like a disease, he says. He's like another person." Moedjid was sweating now. "That's why the good God made the rule that women were not to walk around displaying themselves to all and sundry, arousing these temptations and these desires—indeed, it's like a disease." He loosened his collar. "It makes me uncomfortable to be here in Tunis and see the things I see, walking around on the streets. I feel ill, if the truth must be known. I think tomorrow, with me, it's phweet! Back to Algiers."

Then he brightened. "But I made some inquiries for you and I found a *molluk* who is eager to instruct you in Islam."

A *molluk*, I learned, was the same as a mullah, a low-level Muslim cleric. I wanted nothing less than "instruction" in Islam at that point, but I could not be rude to Moedjid: I had to keep the appointment he had set up for me. So I followed a go-between into the Medina of Tunis, another crowded labyrinth of dark stalls. The *molluk* owned a big store catering to tourists—blankets, clothes, and souvenirs. He had assistants to take care of business. He sat in a private office, removed from the hurly-burly of commerce.

He was a stern figure in a red fez, this *molluk*. Actually, *stern* doesn't cover it. He wore a mean snarl that made me nervous, particularly after the go-between departed. He stared at me balefully for several long, uneasy minutes. Then he broke into speech.

"I will tell you about Islam. It is the law of the universe, and not just for Muslims. It is the law that establishes the reason for the feminine and the reason for the masculine. It is the law that describes for each its duties, for each its place."

To him, in short, the core of the religion was the separation of the sexes.

"The Day of Judgment," he went on ferociously, "starts now. If you do good, surely good will come to you. If you do bad, surely you will receive punishment. If you are an atheist, you will fall into hell and never get out." He held a lighted candle out to me. "Put your hands in this flame. The heat of the fire of Earth is only the *smoke* of the fire of hell. Smoke is white and fire is red, but the fire of hell is black. God is great, however, God is compassionate, He will forgive your sins. Well? Are you ready to become a Muslim?"

I had all the equipment I needed to say yes. I knew enough suras, verses from the Koran, to say my prayers. I knew more than enough about Islam. Yes was all I needed to say to get out of there. On that train to Algiers, I had blurted it out quickly enough, but here, where I felt no immediate danger, my heart grew stubborn. I couldn't say yes because it might be a lie, and I couldn't lie—because I was a Muslim.

The *molluk* frowned. "You doubt me?" He turned in his seat and pointed at a rickety bookcase that contained about twenty dusty old volumes. "Do you see these books?"

"Yes. What about them?"

He paused for dramatic effect, then delivered the impressive news: *"I have read every one of them."*

I had read that many books since leaving New York.

He began to describe hell to me, and as he spoke his living image superimposed itself on my memory of the second-grade religion teacher in Kabul, the one who made me believe I would murder my parents because I had stolen a dime.

"It's not too late to start a clean life," the *molluk* assured me. "God will still accept even you. There is an angel hovering above your left shoulder, recording your misdeeds, and another above your right shoulder, recording your good deeds. When the Judgment trumpet sounds, the records will be placed on the scales of justice, and if the scale tips to the right, you will be saved, but if it tips to the left, you are doomed! That's right, and when you die and you're laid in your grave, an angel will jump on your chest and say, 'Who is your God?' And you must say, 'I believe in the one true God, who has no relatives, kin, or copies. I believe in the one true God,' you must say, and the angel will ask, 'Who speaks for Him?' and you must say, 'Muhammad!' If you can't answer these questions, hellfire will surely consume you. And when the end is approaching, Jesus Christ will descend upon the Earth, and then the whole world will yield to Islam at last. Yes! And there will be great upheaval and humanity will be destroyed and nothing will move or stir across the face of the Earth for thirty-three years. Then Judgment Day will dawn and the dead will all rise from their graves and each one will go before God, and it will be time to answer questions. And there will be no place to hide when that day dawns. The mountains will be leveled and the seas will be filled, and God will find you! And when you are before God, don't imagine that you can play your tricks, because God can read what is written inside your flesh, that's right. It is all written inside your flesh! Each one must answer for his deeds, each one! And then if you go to heaven, you will be thirty-three years old, the age of Christ when he left the Earth. And everyone in heaven will be thirty-three years old, even the children. Well, how about it, are you going to become a Muslim? Are you ready?"

"I have to think about it," I stammered.

"You have no time for that. You could die tonight. Make up your mind now!" He leaned forward, fixed me with his ferocious gaze, and began to intone a verse from the Koran, punctuating his recitation with stabbing gestures. His voice rose and fell, from a wail to a whisper and back, and the whole time he recited, he was gazing at me as if he were speaking to me in English, as if he assumed I could understand every word he was saying. I didn't know whether to nod, look interested, look blank, or just wait patiently. Finally, he brought his recitation to a close and said triumphantly, "Now! Are you becoming a Muslim or not?"

"I won't say yes just to make you happy. I think God would not want to me to say yes unless I were sure in my heart."

He grunted and stood up. He had done his best. I was intractable. "All right. Go. No man knows his fate. You could die tonight. Then you'll wish you had become a Muslim here in my office. But then it will be too late! Good-bye."

As I staggered out, I glanced at my watch and saw that I had been closeted with the *molluk* for nearly two hours.

MICHELLE

IN PARIS, American Express replaced my stolen checks in fifteen minutes and I was back in business. Yes, I could launch into the cold unknown once more.

No, on second thought, I couldn't. I needed to pause for rest and warmth.

I went to the Poste Restante. Why should I have expected a letter from Debby at this point? Her letters were accumulating in Oran now. Or if she had never gotten my letters from Morocco and was going on the original itinerary, she was writing to me in Cairo. But I was banking on the telepathy of true love. When the postmaster came back and shook his head, I felt forgotten. What was going on with Debby?

I went walking on the rue Rivoli, bathed in the late-afternoon light and the loneliness of being in Paris by myself, and in the stinging memories of my last time through this city fifteen years earlier, with my mother and siblings, when we were escaping to America. That time, Paris had felt like pure adventure. This time, true adventure felt like the thing I had left behind when I waved good-bye to Debby in the San Francisco airport. Those sunlit days at the Valencia Street house seemed like such an abstraction now, removed from me not by miles or days but dimensions, a distance immeasurable in space and time. Had there ever been a place called 1049 Valencia Street? Had Debby ever been real?

Reason said yes, but the heart was not so sure. Traveling can erase everything except the present, and turn the present into a hallucination.

I knew one person my age in Paris, though—knew her well, in fact; knew the warmth of her arms, the luxury of her body, her sumptuous breasts. Michelle had come to San Francisco on vacation the year before, and we had met through mutual friends. As soon as I set eyes upon her, I had sinned in my heart. Why should I deny it? God prefers that you admit these things. I was totally charmed by her halting English. I took her to dinner, and after that, we spent a few delightful weeks together before she returned to Paris.

She lived in the suburbs somewhere. I managed to find her number, call her, and get directions. The Metro got me to her neighborhood in twenty minutes flat. I walked from the station to her apartment on a cobblestone street, past quaint European stores: a butcher, a sausage maker, a bakery, a vegetable merchant. It struck me that in America, all these shops would be part of the local Safeway. In Afghanistan, they'd all be separate, but the streets would be raw earth trampled to powder by generations of bare feet. I didn't know who was approaching her apartment, an Afghan or an American.

Michelle hugged me hard and treated me to some snails (for which I was only moderately grateful). Then she made me a substantial French dinner in her tiny kitchen and we ate, and we chatted in French, and we listened to Mozart. We drank wine.

Add the window dressing: late night, outskirts of Paris, big pillows on the floor, music seeping through the windows from other apartments, Eurorock from one direction, a Gallic balladeer from another. And the softened cheese, and the red curtains. And long-legged Michelle in tight pants and a soft sweater.

It got to be midnight finally. The bottle of wine stood mostly empty. We were sitting across a table from each other, leaning close in candlelight. But as Michelle's mood and body language moved forcefully toward sex, I took note of my own intentions and saw not a decision in the making, but a decision already made. "I have to go."

"*Non, non,* Tamim. You have to stay."

"I might get locked out of my hotel."

"You can stay with me. In the morning, I will drive you back to your hotel."

"I can't do that. There is . . . someone else now."

"Ah!" Michelle considered this information with proper, serious respect. "You have promised to be faithful to her?"

"Well, no," I admitted. "No promises yet. But—"

"*Bien. Mais . . .*" Michelle remained charmingly in the dark, a sophisticated Parisian woman of the world, baffled by my reticence. "You know her intention? While you are gone, you know she will be faithful to you?"

Well, no, I didn't even know that for sure. Debby and I had uttered nothing explicit about monogamy, and we were still so close to the sixties, a time when monogamy was not the default mode, especially in the counterculture.

"I have decided to be faithful."

"*Alors.*" Michelle processed what I had said. I was trying to process it, too. "*Eh bien,*" she said. "You don't want to harm your relationship with this woman. . . ."

"*Exactement!*"

"But she is not here. She is thousands of miles away . . . and for us, it's just tonight. It's nothing serious. How could it harm your relationship, you and me . . . tonight?"

My body was telling me she had a point. But I was not wrestling with a choice. No, the choice was made. I just wanted to formulate why. And I discovered the thought as I uttered it painstakingly in French. "It doesn't matter what she knows or doesn't know. It only matters what I know."

And uttering those words revealed to me a deep and consequential belief. Debby could not release me from my vow by betraying my confidence, because my stance was not contingent. This was not a contract. A "believer" (as subscribers to the notion of a personal God sometimes describe themselves) might have cast the same thought by saying, "It doesn't matter what she knows: Even when I'm alone, I'm known by God and subject to His judgment." An Afghan friend once said to me, "I believe in God because otherwise, for whom should I be good?" But for me, as I discovered that night, "for whom" doesn't enter into it. The Good constitutes its own imperative. In other words, I am a Mu'tazilite.

And that was the night I married Debby, because even though she wasn't there, that was the night I took the vow that includes the phrase "till death do us part."

THE BUS TO TURKEY

THE BOSFOR TURIZM BUS COMPANY operated out of a dingy storefront and ran one bus a week from Paris to Istanbul, leaving Thursday morning. I had caught a cold, but I dragged my phlegmy body to the Bosfor station, where I joined about twenty other passengers, all of them Turks.

The two drivers were also Turkish. One was obviously the chief, the other his distant second in command. The chief, a sturdy guy with a brisk air of competence, did most of the driving. His deputy, a pudgy, overgrown boy, spent most of his time sleeping, eating, and cracking ribald jokes with one of the passengers, a crude, stout woman with greedy features who, I later learned, belonged to Turkey's neo-Nazi movement, the National Action party.

The bus was a good deal: two hundred dollars for a

round-trip ticket, plus thirty-five dollars a night for hotels and meals along the way.

About midafternoon, we started to climb into the mountains, and by gray of dusk, we found ourselves on the huge white slabs of the Alps. At the Swiss border, things started to get a little weird: The border police wouldn't let us cross. The passengers buzzed over this in Turkish, but I didn't know any Turkish, so I could only guess why a bus on a regular schedule would have trouble with a routine border crossing. We drove to a second crossing, were refused, then a third. Refused again. Each time, the bus had to be turned around on the narrow road, which involved a Laurel and Hardy procedure, with the number-two bus driver shouting instructions from the roadside while the commander backed the bus into snowbanks, scraped other cars, and barely missed hitting pedestrians. The passengers crowded to the windows, shouting cacophonous advice. At the fourth border post, the police reluctantly let us across, but the policeman was speaking French, and I was close enough to overhear what he said: "This road doesn't go to Istanbul."

"*Rien* problem. *Rien* problem! Geneva!" the driver cried. Soon, however, he discovered his mistake and pulled over to pore over maps. The passengers hovered close to offer opinions. Finally, the driver revved the engine again. I wondered if my bus drivers might be escaped lunatics in stolen uniforms.

The feeling deepened with the snow. The Swiss highway

patrol stopped us and warned us not to go any farther. I thought I heard something about an avalanche up ahead, but I wasn't sure. Stranded vehicles lined the road and traffic snarled the downhill lane, but our drivers managed to weasel through and keep going.

The next time we were stopped, one of the passengers took over as translator. He was an elderly, flamboyant lawyer with a magnificent shock of wavy silver hair flowing out from under his Russian-style brown fur cap. His French was little more than a collection of phrases and sayings strung together at random. *"Mes amis . . . pardon! Moi aussi! Rien de tout!"* he shouted at the officers. *"Touts les passagers! C'est la vie! Allons, allons, mes camarades! Istanbul!"* But he delivered his French-sounding nonsense with all the oratorical éclat of a Clarence Darrow defending the theory of evolution.

Finally, wearily, the Swiss police officers waved us through, and as we continued up the highway, the passengers burst into song.

Walls of snow on either side began choking the road down to one narrow corridor. Night fell, but the passengers carried on. Every one of them, it seemed, was smoking Gauloises, Gitanes, or stronger Turkish cigarettes, but the neo-Nazi peasant woman would not allow the windows to be opened, for fear of catching cold. Instead, she sprayed the whole interior of the bus with cologne.

At the Italian border, police officers stopped us again; I heard more talk of an avalanche ahead. They directed us into a large covered parking lot, where dozens of parked trucks were running their motors for warmth, putting out dense plumes of exhaust. Outside, the air had become a shimmering tapestry of falling snow.

Now the neo-Nazi peasant banged the roof vents open. Carbon monoxide poured in, mixing with the fumes and gases already in the bus. Everyone began to cough, and two or three people jumped up to spray the air with cologne. Surrendering to hyperbole, I told the driver, "If you don't move this bus, we're all going to die!" But he replied philosophically, "It doesn't matter to me. I am a bachelor."

We slept on and off. At dawn, before the authorities woke up, our drivers put the bus in gear and we went barreling up the road. Within ten minutes, we came to a wall of impacted snow—the avalanche at last.

We parked and waited. The minutes passed. The hours passed.

At one point, the man across the aisle from me struck up a conversation. He wore glasses, and his pale forehead rose high into his thinning hair. He spoke good English, and his jeans and sport shirt bespoke an easy familiarity with the West. He had lived in France for eight years, but he was Turkish, he assured me, and this was his first time back since he'd left.

"I'm Oooor."

"Ooor?" I said.

"No, Oooor.

"Oooor?" I searched for the nuance of pronunciation he was trying to get across, but I couldn't hear it. Finally, he spelled his name: Uger.

"It's a soft *g*," he explained. "Oooor."

Uger spent the next eight hours telling me what a troubled country Turkey was. Prices were doubling every year, 3 million people were out of work, and Turkey had no welfare system. "A neo-Nazi party got ten percent in the last election, and it's run by a man who recommends *Mein Kampf* to his followers," Uger said bitterly, "and on the Left, there are at least one hundred groups. The universities are deeply polarized, and most students carry pistols. On top of all that, the country is now plagued by a growing Islamic fundamentalist movement!"

He had me sitting up. Hey, maybe this could be my story. Turkey sounded like an explosion waiting to happen—about to be overrun by neo-Nazis or Muslim fundamentalists. Events had moved too fast for me in the Islam story, but with Turkey, I would be ahead of the news. When the pressure cooker blew, I would be ready with my notes and research. Suddenly, a fresh wind was blowing through my life.

I was about to press Uger for further details, when something crashed onto the roof. Chunks of snow were falling on us! The driver hastily backed the bus up. In fact, he traveled in reverse down that slippery, winding one-lane mountain road for miles, until he reached a restaurant, where we went inside to have café crèmes and eat oranges and chat in happy clusters around the checker-clothed tables. The lawyer was ordering whiskeys for a punk kid he'd taken under his wing, and this fifteen-year-old was downing them one after another, looking agog and pleased. "Ah, friend," the lawyer told me in English, "life is a romance of women . . . song . . . and wine!" Zorba the Turk.

It took us three days and nights to reach Istanbul, and I remember the calm elegance of our stop in Yugoslavia, where the hotel served us a gourmet meal of lentil soup, polenta, rabbit, and Chianti. I had never expected such luxury in a Communist country. Years later, I had trouble believing that ethnic cleansing had overwhelmed this very region.

But then, I never thought ethnic cleansing would reach its climax in Afghanistan.

ISTANBUL

I MADE GOOD FRIENDS with Uger during the journey, and when we arrived in Istanbul, he invited me to stay with him and make his apartment my base while I gathered my Turkey story. His apartment was a large, dreary place on the fifth floor of a crumbling old six-story building, all the other floors of which seemed to be vacant. Uger's apartment had crystal chandeliers and ornate Versailles-style furnishings, including a grand piano and fancy Oriental carpets, but the plaster was cracking off the walls, the ceilings were dark with ancient soot, and the upholstery on the fancy chairs was tattering. This apartment, like all others in Istanbul, had no electricity from 7 a.m. till noon; water flowed in the pipes for only two hours a day; and the central heating system barely managed to get the radiators warm to the touch. But we were lucky to have any heat at all, for most of Turkey had none in this, the coldest winter in ten years.

After a nap that first day, I went out for a look at the neighborhood. Two p.m. looked like 7 p.m. The sky was opaque, and an icy wind drove the rain almost parallel to the ground. The streets were crowded, however. I saw hundreds of vendors trying to sell worthless trinkets from handcarts—cheap watchbands, cigarette lighters, plastic trinkets. Who on earth would buy such things at a time of economic crisis? The sight of these vendors hunched over their carts, blowing into their cupped hands for warmth, made me want to cry.

I saw, with a lurch of dread, that ahead of me on the sidewalk, someone had fallen down. Then I realized that the person—man or woman, I could not tell—was crawling through the mud, moaning, and pushing a cup. The crowds parted and flowed around the ancient beggar, and a few people dropped coins into the cup as they hurried past. But Turkish liras were so worthless at this point, according to Uger, that the cost of producing them exceeded the face value of the coins. People were melting them down to make spoons, which they could sell at a profit.

Throughout Istanbul, I could feel a growing desperation about the country's economic tailspin. Every time the lira was devalued, the price of all exported goods went up 30 percent overnight. And the lira was being devalued just about every week. For Uger's class, this meant sinking back down into the Islamic past, down into the Ottoman world they thought they had escaped.

On my walks that week, I kept seeing old men with long beards and berets. They looked like Impressionist painters—like Monet, to be exact. I saw hundreds of these Monets, all over Istanbul. Finally, someone explained to me that these men were fundamentalist Muslims. Turkish law banned religious headgear, but Islamic law forbade men to walk around bareheaded. The Islamists sneaked around the religious headgear law by wearing berets.

I knew that Turkey had undergone a radical change after the Ottoman Empire collapsed, that Atatürk had dismantled the empire and modernized Turkey. But I had never realized how radically he and his cronies had attacked Islam. Turkey had been the seat of the caliphate— the official political center of the Islamic world. The religious schools and scholars, the founts of Islamic law, all were here: the most concentrated nexus of Islam (outside of Arabia and Egypt). And yet Atatürk had managed to squelch Islam utterly, *here* in its heartland. He banned beards. He banned religious headgear. He banned the fez. He banned the flowing clothes the Muslims wore in the Ottoman Empire. He converted the mosques into stables—that's pretty extreme. And he more or less made it stick. Turks had accepted the secular state and transformed their society. A whole layer of educated Turks plaintively called themselves Europeans. As far as I know, nothing like this has happened to Islam anywhere else, ever. Islam has been pushed back by external conquest, but never has it collapsed from within. Wherever it has come, it has stayed. Islam only expands. Except in Turkey.

But now, it seemed, Islam was welling up again even here in Turkey. This country had its share of battle-hardened radical leftists and ferociously fascistic right-wingers—spiritual heirs of Atatürk, who modernized Turkey, yes, and replaced the religious state with a secular one, but not as a liberal move—he and his cronies established a racist, right-wing militarized state whose genocidal attacks on the Armenians presaged the Holocaust in Nazi Germany.

The Islamic movement baffled other Turks. It was neither right-wing in the old sense nor left-wing. No one knew what it was, what to do about it, or where it was going. As a leftist, Uger worried desperately about the new force. For this very reason, he disagreed with me about Afghanistan. When he looked at my country under the Soviet boot, he saw people of his own ideology stamping out the forces he feared and despised in Turkey. To him, the Soviets represented modernism moving Afghanistan out of its reactionary past. Grudgingly, he admitted there might be some sovereignty issues here, and that the Soviets might be committing some human rights violations, but a lot of this, he opined, was probably Western propaganda, and on balance, the conquest of ancient superstition by rational modernism was always a step in the right direction.

I had many of the same elements in my psyche. My family was part of the leading edge of rational secularism in Afghanistan. We were the Westernized ones, as Uger was in Turkish society; and then in American society, I had been a hard-core member of the radical counterculture, a leftist by any measure.

The Soviet invasion had complicated my views, however. In it, I could see only suppression, violence, arrogance, and the utter injustice of foreigners telling Afghans, "We are going to develop you primitive animals." I could not think or talk about Afghan politics without feeling anger and outrage. And every night, I dreamed I had inadvertently strayed into Afghanistan. The place was always green and pleasant, but the greenery was just a mask stretched over terror. Nightmare oozed from the very pores of the landscape.

But our disagreement didn't sour our friendship, because Uger had no passion about Afghanistan. He didn't actually care who ruled it or how. To him, it was just some Podunk, a nothing place out in nowhere, and he was willing to say, "Well, maybe" to anything I proposed.

One night, Uger took me to dinner at his cousin Fahir's house. Fahir was a professor of nuclear physics at Bosphorus University. His apartment had the same air of faded splendor as Uger's. On TV, Prime Minister Demirel and opposition leader Ecevit were holding a press conference— more like a duel, as it turned out.

Over the background mumbling of the TV, we talked about Turkey's problems. Fahir said, "The Turkish police are confiscating about thirty-five thousand weapons a year now. Where do all these arms come from? No one knows. And where does the money come from? Bank robberies, extortion rackets, drug smuggling! The rackets even oper-te among Turkish workers abroad. If a factory in France or Italy has one hundred Turkish workers, a representative from the Right comes there to collect for a fund to fight some alleged threat to Turkey. Those who refuse to pay into the fund are harassed, beaten, even killed."

I asked how the inflation made them feel. I asked because I was remembering a burst of inflation in San Francisco when bread shot from eighty-nine cents to a dollar and gas went from fifty to fifty-five cents in a matter of weeks. Debby had said the rising prices frightened her, and I knew what she meant. But that was laughable inflation compared to the nightmare Turkey was going through.

Fahir's wife said, "It would be different if this were happening only to me. If this were just my personal crisis, I think I could cope with my feelings better; I could stay calm, hope for better, work to get out of my predicament. But what's happening now is happening to everybody, so everyone has this feeling that things are out of control. The paranoia is leaking out, and you feel it everywhere—it's in the air; it soaks into you and makes it so hard to keep your fear under control."

During the press conference, Ecevit accused the Demirel government of selling out to private interests. Then Demirel said he was only trying to sort out the mess left behind by Ecevit.

Fahir laughed bitterly. "Each government accuses the other because neither one can admit it is helpless."

Uger shook his head sadly. "It was criminal of the Demirel government to lift price controls. Criminal!"

"It's not so simple," said Fahir. "During Ecevit's time,

the price of cooking oil was controlled at forty-five lira per liter, but you couldn't find any in the stores, because it cost sixty lira to produce. The manufacturers sold everything they produced to the black market, and you could get it there for a hundred and twenty lira. When Demirel came back, he lifted the price controls, and suddenly there was plenty of oil in the regular stores, selling at ninety lira per liter. For us, a saving of thirty lira."

"That's the price you pay for having a capitalistic system," said Uger. "The only real solution is to open up the Turkish border and invite the Red Army in, so we can have a second Afghanistan."

"Well," said Fahir's wife. "There's the third solution. We can all buy religious headgear and return to Islam."

Everybody laughed.

"No," she said, "seriously. I can see why some people go that way. It doesn't seem like any human power can solve this problem. It's going to take God Almighty. The laws of nature have to be suspended. It's the only hope."

We returned through the white and silent streets to Uger's apartment. It was 1 a.m. and the streets were deserted. Then Monet approached us through the dark. "Hey, brother, do you know the time?" he called out.

Uger picked up his pace without answering. When we were out of the man's earshot, he said, "That's an old trick."

I didn't get it. "What's the trick?"

"They ask you for the time. When you stop, they mug you."

THE EMBASSY

THE NEXT WEEK, I went to a travel agency to ask how much a bus ticket to Pakistan would cost. The answer? Forty dollars. The catch? The bus went through Iran. It threw me into a torment of indecision. To be within forty dollars of Pakistan and not go seemed unbearable!

In line at the post office (where I still went every day), I fell into conversation with a British guy. He told me he was boarding a bus for Tehran that night.

"You don't have any qualms?" I asked him.

"I've talked to many people who have just come through. They had no problem."

"Any Americans among them?"

"Ha-ha," he said. After a moment of silence, he added, "No." After another beat: "Actually, the first thing anyone asks you in there is whether you're an American."

"What do they do if you are?"

He shrugged, and laughed again, nervously this time. "I haven't met any Americans coming out."

I went back to Uger's apartment to ponder my options. Would it really be a risk? My new Turkish friends considered me insane. "They'll tie you up, blindfold you, throw you in a dark room, and later shoot you," they said. "Look what they've done to the ones they've already caught!"

The trouble was, I couldn't trust my gut feeling. My gut didn't have a good track record. Every decision I had made on this trip had been wrong. In fact, I didn't even know what my gut feeling was. The papers said the Communists were torturing people like my father in Afghanistan. The map said Pakistan was a lot closer to Afghanistan than Turkey was. When Riaz was in that area, my father had managed to get out, and they met in Delhi. That was before the Soviet tanks, but still. The travel agent said I could get as close to my father as Riaz had gotten, for just forty dollars.

I had to check it out. I made my way to the Iranian embassy, which I found surrounded by Iranian students. When I say "students," I don't mean they were enrolled in any school. They just matched the age and look of the young men who are called "students" everywhere in the world. These ones were milling about outside the embassy for no particular reason except that they were so excited about events in Iran.

I struck up a conversation with one of these young men and presented my bio to him in Farsi, which I spoke with a convincing Afghan accent. As I laid it out, I finally realized something: All this time, I had thought I was pretending to be on a personal quest in order to pursue my real goal of bagging a story. Now I realized I was pretending to be a journalist in order to pursue my real goal of exploring my roots, nailing down my identity. From Morocco to Istanbul, I had been telling the truth. . . .

When I finished, the Iranian fellow had tears in his eyes, not because I was eloquent, but because he was already brimming with emotion around these issues of exile and the homeland and returning to the ways of the father. He grasped my hand and made an attempt to hug me, which I resisted, and he said, "We are brothers! You and me! Afghans and Iranians! Brothers!"

"Do you think I can get a visa to travel through Iran, then?"

"Are you joking? What would we deny to our brother Muslim? Come in. I know people at the embassy. Come with me." He took my hand and led me up the stairs, into a long hall crowded with more chattering young people. He took me into a long sparse room where another student type was sitting behind a desk piled high with documents and papers.

My good sponsor introduced me to the boy behind the desk. "This is Tamim Ansary, our brother Afghan, long lost in the wilderness of the West, now returning to his home, and he needs a visa. Tell him, Tamim."

The guy behind the desk looked at me curiously, and I felt his warmth, his interest and invitation. As I told my story, my eyes stayed dry, but my voice trembled. I told him everything I had told the fellow outside, but more this time, much more. I really let go, and extemporized from the heart. I found my eloquence. Again, I sparked an astounding reaction. The new guy slammed his palm on the desk and half-stood out of his chair to shake my hand. "Where is your passport?" he cried. "Give it here; I will stamp it for you at once—my brother!"

I cleared my throat and said, still in Farsi, "One small problem, though. I am traveling, you see, on an American passport."

Every expression turned exactly upside down; each smile became its mirroring frown.

The boy behind the desk addressed me in thickly accented English. "What is your name? Where do you want to go?"

I answered him in Farsi. "I just told you. My name is Tamim and—"

"No. Talk in American," he said. "Tell me where you want to go. What do you want from this embassy?"

Speaking in Farsi again, I said, "What I just told you is the truth. I swear it."

"Tell me again," he sneered. "Swear it in the American language."

It struck me suddenly that the Iranian embassy was, technically speaking, Iranian soil. And that the door behind me was shut. And that the hall outside was crowded with excited Iranian revolutionary patriots. And so was the lobby. And so were the stairs, and the street outside.

I swallowed and obeyed the order. I told him who I was,

where I was from, and how I had left Afghanistan, the whole story—in English. He didn't interrupt, just folded his arms, leaned back, and watched, but without actually listening. He was merely taking pleasure in making me perform.

I finished by saying, "However, if you can't give me a visa—" My passport was on the table. I picked it up, put it in my pocket, and reverted to Farsi again. "Okay, but you're not being very hospitable."

"Don't speak to me in Farsi," he screamed in English. He jumped to his feet. "You American! You speak to me in American!"

I said in Farsi, "*Kho*. It's your decision. If you want me to go, I will go." It was not at all clear they wanted me to go. I had the feeling they wanted me to stay. But I sure as hell wanted to go. What stupid impulse convinced me to come in here at all? I wondered. I turned and walked to the door, affecting unhurried ease, the way one does in a yard with an unchained dog. The two men just watched me. When I opened the door, the one who had sponsored me hissed, "Yes! Go! Bastard!"

For a true macho journalist, this would have been merely the beginning. A true MJ would have found some way to sneak across the border disguised as a truck driver. But I was not a macho journalist, it turned out. I went back to Uger's apartment and lay in my opulently furnished room and listened to my heartbeat.

That night, Uger took me to a dinner party at the house

of another Turkish couple about our age. Everyone spoke English for once. Over coffee, late that evening, Uger started talking about his mother's death. I knew the story, but on this night, he opened up about his feelings, and he stirred me. "It has really changed my consciousness," he confided. "Another immovable immortal has disappeared from the landscape. I feel my own fragility now, and the size of the cosmos. My mother was in completely good health all these years. We wrote letters back and forth. The last one was just two weeks before she died. On the twenty-seventh of December, she got sick and had to be taken to the hospital. No one knew it was serious at the time, but they sent me a telegram on the twenty-eighth to let me know that she was ill. The telegram didn't reach me till the thirtieth, by which time she had already died. I didn't know that, of course, and I called Turkey on New Year's Eve to wish her happy holidays and inquire how she was feeling. Strangers answered the phone and told me she was dead. I had been saving for ten years to buy a good stereo system, and only a few days earlier I had finally bought it. I had it set up at home and was going to try it out for the first time that night. But after hearing about my mother, I looked at that expensive set, the tape deck, the receiver, the turntable, the speakers—and I wanted to throw it out the window. Because it struck me for the first time that human relationships are the only things that are utterly irreplaceable. If I threw that stereo set into the street, I could eventually get another one. Even if I never really succeeded in saving that much money again, still, it was replaceable in theory. But a human relationship, when it's gone, it's finished. And anything you might feel sorry for, there is no chance to correct it. And anything you planned to do together, that's finished, too. There is no replacing a relationship."

This was followed by a moment of awed silence.

More coffee was served, Turkish coffee, thick and sweet, with inches of sediment at the bottom of the cup.

Then I said, "In America, as far as I can tell, human relationships pass out of one's life all the time. Eventually, you build up a different attitude, because you have to. No matter how you cling to the people you love, you realize that there is a last time you will see anyone. One way or another, sooner or later, the good-bye moment always comes. At some level, you have to ask what difference it makes if good-bye comes tomorrow or twenty years from now. It's good-bye all the same. After a while, you learn to let go and keep yourself open to new friendship, new friendships, all the time new friendships. I guess at some level, I have come to believe that is the only viable way to approach life."

But as I spoke those words, I remembered Hungria coming back to us the night before we left for Lashkargah. The memory of all my friends in San Francisco flared inside me like an ache, and I realized the truth of what Uger was saying: My irreplaceable loved ones gave my life whatever value it had.

Turkey was a box canyon. From there, I couldn't go anywhere, except back. But I couldn't go back yet, because I still had money—enough money to stay in Turkey for quite a while, and since I didn't know when I would be this way again, I couldn't waste the opportunity. I had to stay till my money ran out. Didn't I?

I took a trip through Anatolia, with a stop in Ankara and a week on the Mediterranean coast, but felt too disheartened to enjoy it. The coastal city of Antalya was stunningly pretty, perched on cliffs facing a Mediterranean of unbearable blue. Sidewalk cafés and open-air restaurants abounded. The air was feather-light, soft, and springlike. The only thing missing was Debby, but that was everything.

I tried to write. Thousands of miles on the ground, months on the road, hundreds of conversations with Muslims, and I had not shaped a single coherent article. Without English around me, my head felt empty, as if my thoughts were only internalized versions of my conversations. All I had written were letters, passionate letters to Debby, which she had never answered and which seemed, therefore, in retrospect, dangerously mawkish.

The only image I could muster vividly of home was Debby's face. I had the photos I had shot of her on the California coast. I had taken to carrying them around in my jacket and pulling them out from time to time, just as my guide Mohammed in Tangier did with that note from the American girl.

I went back to Istanbul.

THE TRUE BELIEVER

O N MY SECOND DAY BACK, I strolled past a bookstore with some English-language books about
Islam displayed in the window. I went inside
to browse, and one of the proprietors, speaking broken
English, tried to explain the concept of One God.

"I know," I told him with good-humored impatience. "I
know. I am a Muslim myself, from Afghanistan."

This news created a great stir among the young men
working in the bookstore. They surrounded me like
friendly puppies, offering me books and gesticulating
wildly. "Afghanistan bang bang! *Mujahideen!* Hikmatyar!"
they cried, naming the leader of one of the seven main
anti-Soviet mujahideen parties in Pakistan.

"Hikmatyar good?" I asked.

"Hikmatyar good! Engineer Gulbuddin Hikmatyar!"

Then one of them broke into excited chatter. An idea

had struck him. The others approved. They grasped my arm and led me through the store, out the back, into an alley, down a maze of narrow streets, and finally into a kind of apartment that opened directly off the street, like a storefront, but with several back rooms. All these rooms were unfurnished except the one farthest back, which had a washtub, a wooden table, and several skeletal chairs under a bare bulb hanging from the ceiling by a frayed chord. I admit that something about that tableau made me picture myself under the bare bulb, bound to my chair, blindfolded and gagged.

"Hikmatyar! Hikmatyar!" they kept chanting as they pushed me down into one of the chairs. Then several of them left the room, while the rest hovered around me, beaming.

Presently, a new man came into the room. He was older than the rest—about my age. He wore a dark three-piece pin-striped business suit that looked expensive. He had a coal black beard and shining dark eyes and a dark complexion, and a certain muscular charisma that I felt instantly. In perfect English, he told me his name was Abdul Qayum.

"You're American," I exclaimed.

"Not anymore," he replied. "Now I am a Muslim."

He was, I learned, a college-educated Puerto Rican from New York, named Alberto once upon a time. He was from my world. He'd done all the usual sixties things: lived in communes, opposed the Vietnam War, smoked grass. He knew rock musicians, and, like many of our generation, he'd searched the spiritual bazaars for a religion that fit his hunger.

"You mean like Buddhism? All that?"

"Yeah." He laughed. "Gurus, meditation, I did it all. But I wasn't satisfied. I wasn't making any progress, and the reason was, none of them had a social project. All they offered was another way of getting high."

I was intrigued, because he was echoing an opinion of my own. "Okay. So how did you get into Islam?"

"I met some Sufis in London," he said.

He didn't have to explain the term to me. I knew all about Sufism, the traditional mystical branch of Islam. Typically, a Sufi brotherhood forms around a sheikh, a teacher who knows how to transcend this world and experience God directly. Most of the great poets of Persian literature have been Sufis. My own great-great-grandfather was a Sufi poet. In the past several hundred years, Islam has expanded mainly through the proliferation of Sufi brotherhoods.

"I was immediately attracted to the personalities of the Sufi elders in this group," Qayum went on rapturously. "The old men, they have a sweetness that goes beyond anything I've ever met, just an incredible radiance of heart."

After London, Qayum had gone to Spain, where he ran out of money. "But it was no problem. I found another Muslim brotherhood that took me in. That's how it is, once you become a Muslim. Everywhere you go, you find community. One day, a Sufi sheikh came to this brotherhood and said, 'Which of you wants to go to Turkey to study Islam formally?' I raised my hand, and the sheikh gave me a thousand dollars on the spot. I came to Istanbul, where I met the Issik brotherhood who run the bookstore you stumbled into. They took me in and they even bought me this suit I'm wearing." But it wasn't just the personalities of the elders, he declared. "The instant I learned about Islam, I felt that finally, after all my seeking, I was face-to-face with an ideology that struck home, that just plain sounded right."

"And what was it that sounded so right?" I asked.

He blistered me with a long discourse. He didn't mind my taking notes, since he saw himself as a teacher, so I can give you the gist of what he said now, more than twenty years later.

"Prophet Muhammad, peace be upon him, said there are only two social systems in the world, that of the unbelievers and that of Islam. So capitalism and communism are actually the same system, with different aspects exaggerated. The only difference is in their economic doctrine: In one, the state is the capitalist; in the other, individuals are the capitalists. But as far as education goes, as far as culture, as far as politics, social life, and moral life, as far as sexual relations and the ultimate objectives of the legal system, what people are living for, these systems are basically indistinguishable from each other. A respected professor in Peking University is a respected professor in Moscow is a respected professor at Harvard. And even in their economic systems, there is a common basis, for in all these countries, the economy is founded on banking, and Islam is the enemy of banking. Islam prohibits usury. You can't charge interest in Islam, and the whole international banking system is founded on interest, which is to say usury, which is to say exploitation.

"The social project of Islam is inconceivably superior to all others because there is no bureaucracy in Islam—none. There is no need for leaders or the apparatus of state, because a community of Muslims functions without any such need. In the time of the Prophet, there were no police in the community. When someone was harming someone else, any member of the community who happened to be present functioned as the police. They leaped in to protect the victim. The trial was held immediately, and the punishment dealt out in minutes. I have friends who have been in jail for over a year, just waiting for their trial. That is barbaric! There were no soldiers in the perfect Islamic community. When soldiers were needed, every man was a soldier. When the problem was solved, the army ceased to exist.

"You hear about Islamic culture, the magnificent city of Baghdad, the wealth and splendor of Córdoba and Granada—that was not Islam. Perhaps Islam existed at that time, but if so, it was being practiced in some obscure alley or in some neighborhood. And the same is true today. Saudi Arabia is not a Muslim country. All you have to do is look at how the rulers live and how they treat the people. The Saudi state is not an example of Islam, because the rulers use Islam to tyrannize the people. But in Islam, there can be no tyranny, because everyone is the same. No one has legitimate power over anyone else.

"In Communist and capitalist societies, there are three important words—the *state,* the *people,* the *leader.* But in Islam, these words are irrelevant—because they are abstractions used to justify exploitation. In the non-Muslim world, political organization is from the top down. In Islam, it is from the bottom up. Every individual is free from the tyranny of other individuals because all are obedient to the single law of Allah, and nothing else rules. After the individual, there is only the *jamiat*—the community. And the community freely and democratically elects an emir. But the emir does not, himself, have any power. He is like the vacuum in the middle of the cyclone, the central point around which whirls the power of the community. He cannot make his own laws or enforce his own wishes, because he derives his authority solely from the Koran and the *sharia.* When he departs from these, he is no longer the emir, and the people have no duty to obey him."

"The *sharia,*" I said. "Yes, that's what people have trouble with. It seems like such a harsh legal code. The cutting off of hands—"

"You have to understand that the *sharia* is much more than a legal system," he said, interrupting me. "All the elements of the *sharia*—the rules of inheritance, the punishments set down for different crimes, the proscriptions about food and dress and all the rest of it—are like markers. They show where the road is. That's what *sharia* means—it is the way. The rules are not restrictive, as people think, because within the *sharia*, a Muslim is free. So long as the people of a community stay on the road, they progress toward the light. When they stray from the road, that's when they get into brambles and thorns.

"So the Islamic community has a *sharia*, but this is founded on an absolute reality, which is in the heart of each Muslim, and this absolute reality is Allah. The social project comes out of the individual project of each Muslim, which is to attain the quality of the heart that makes one a good Muslim. The *sharia* is the outward expression of this project. And prayer is the inward expression. There is no room for improvisation in Islam.

"The *sharia* does indeed say cut off the hands of thieves, but the *sharia* is not a law directed at punishing an individual for his crimes; it is a guideline for the whole community. It is directed toward making the community function well. So when the *sharia* is really in place, no hands are cut off, because there is no stealing!

"Shall I give you Islam in a single phrase? Greet the guest and feed the stranger.

"Throughout the Muslim world, you know, these brotherhoods exist that have no formal structure and no relation to the state. They have no bureaucracy and no leader except the sheikh, who is not a ruler, but a spiritual leader, or, better yet, a helper. And although there may be differences between this brotherhood and that, they don't distinguish themselves from the mainstream of Islam. So any member of these brotherhoods has an affectionate feeling toward any other Muslim. You might compare them to American colleges in the sixties. If you were a student then, you went to a particular college, and that was your base. But if you met another student on the road, you didn't have a feeling of college chauvinism. You felt like you were both part of the same big river of experience; you shared attitudes and convictions and experiences, and these allowed you to pool your lot with all your fellow college students."

When he finished his lecture, he pressed some pamphlets on me. "It's all here," he said. "Read these. They will open your eyes. And listen, when you return to England, if you're going through London, look up my brotherhood." He wrote an address and a phone number on a piece of paper. "Ask for Sheikh Zamzama," he added.

"Did you say Zamzama?"

"Yes."

It was the same name I had heard from the lips of the shopkeeper Abdullah at the beginning of my odyssey. Those Moroccans and this Puerto Rican fellow had been dazzled by the same light.

By this time, I had finished and abandoned all my books about Islam, as well as my interest in the topic. I was reading the *Odyssey* now, the FitzGerald translation, a copy of which I'd acquired in Paris. What a read! TV should be so flat-out entertaining. Think about the end, when Odysseus comes home and bunks with the swineherd and touches base with Telemachus. And we see him slowly moving in on the suitors, giving them every chance to reclaim their decency, and we see them inexorably blowing every opportunity, until they have squandered their last claim to salvation, and then the stage is set. Someone once called the movie *Dirty Harry* a "rage-release film." The *Odyssey* strikes me as the granddaddy of rage-release literature. By the time you get to the climactic showdown between Odysseus and the suitors, you're standing on your chair, pumping your fist, and shouting, "Kill!"

That chapter begins with a fantastic passage in which Penelope takes Odysseus's bow out to the great hall, and tells the suitors, Okay, I give up. I'll marry whoever can string this bow. And none of them can. But then Odysseus, disguised as a tramp, says let me try, and that's how he gets the bow in his hands, after which the slaughter begins. The text pretends that Penelope has no idea what she's done, but I don't buy it. When Penelope picks up that bow, it's because she knows Odysseus has come home. Without a word, she swings into action as his partner and his equal.

I saw a great similarity between Odysseus and myself. Of course, there were some crucial differences, too. He was a resourceful hero who prevailed in his mighty quest. I was a wide-eyed naïf whose wooden horse the Trojans were even now using for firewood while Helen discussed daycare options for the kids with her husband Paris.

How, then, were we similar, Odysseus and I? We both

had a Penelope. The telepathy of true love had kicked in at last, and somehow I knew that Debby was unraveling a sweater every night. It wasn't a premonition that took me to the post office that day. I went every day. But this time, for the first time in my trip, I had mail—and not just one letter, but two.

One was from Riaz. He wanted me to know he'd heard from our father, who was still in Kabul, not happy, but safe.

The other letter was from Debby. I read it standing on the sidewalk somewhere in downtown Istanbul. She'd been sending letters relentlessly to all the places I said I'd be. But of course I'd never been where I said I would, and so I'd missed them all.

It was five o'clock and the buildings were disgorging workers, who were elbowing one another aside to get on buses. They paid no attention to me and I paid none to them. It had gotten dark, but I just stood there going through the photos by the light from a barrel of burning firewood that some poor guys were using to warm their hands, and I thought, What am I doing here in Istanbul in the cold and dark?

That night, in Homer, I reached the part where Odysseus is finally reunited with Penelope. As Homer put it:

> *Now from his breast into his eyes the ache*
> *of longing mounted, and he wept at last,*
> *his dear wife, clear and faithful, in his arms*
> *longed for*
>   *as the sunwarmed earth is longed for by a swimmer*

spent in rough water where his ship went down
under Poseidon's blows, gale winds and tons of sea.

I pictured myself back in the Valencia Street house with Debby, living with her in that big room that used to be mine alone, waking up with her in the morning, cooking dinners with her and my roommates . . . and my feelings spread to American enthusiasms in general. I would write a novel about my days in Portland . . . explore photography . . . finish my dragon painting . . . sip lattes in San Francisco cafés, disputing philosophy or who had the best first step in basketball with Paul Lobell. . . .

Clearly, my trip was over. No, I didn't get a news story. All I did was learn about myself—that I was not a macho journalist, and that my soul was not on the road or in the East. The Islamic world was someone else's, not mine.

The next morning, I said good-bye to Uger and got on the bus to Paris, leaving my gentle Turkish friends behind in their darkening world. I returned through Paris, London, and New York, to San Francisco. I moved in with Debby and took up my life as one unconflicted soul: Tamim Ansary, American guy.

PART THREE

Forgetting Afghanistan

THE REBEL LEADER

FTER I CAME BACK from the Islamic world, I fell in with a bunch of Afghans in Berkeley. I had met them shortly after moving to San Francisco, but I hadn't hung out with them much, because I'd felt sort of awkward among them; I'd felt I didn't know all the secret handshakes of Afghan culture anymore. They shared references to times and places I had left behind. Often, I didn't get their jokes. My Farsi wasn't that good.

But after I came back, something changed. I think the Soviet invasion drew us together. They had all come over on student visas, never meaning to stay. The invasion clanged the gate shut on them, and now they were trapped in America. I had never intended to go back, but now that I couldn't, it affected me. It was as if some Afghan self inside me woke up and realized it didn't want to die.

One day, one of the Berkeley Afghans came to me and said, "We have to form a committee." His name was Aziz Mujadeddi and he was one of my closest buddies at this time, a big, handsome, athletic fellow with shiny black hair and warm dark eyes. Aziz loved art and painted big canvases filled with surrealistic images. Anytime he got excited, which was every few minutes, he stumbled all over his tongue trying to explain deep thoughts, which no one ever got, because language was not his strong suit.

"What kind of committee?"

"Let's raise money to help the refugees in Pakistan."

He had my attention. Letters from my father were still arriving regularly, and they brought only good news, but that was bad news, because it meant he was writing for the censors. For the most part, he just listed the names of relatives who were fine and who sent salaams. In other news, meat was always plentiful in the bazaars, coal was inexpensive, and the weather was always unseasonably good.

But one day in mid-1980, an anonymous letter hit my mailbox, warning me in block lettering not to come back to Afghanistan. "Everyone is being arrested here. If they catch you listening to BBC, you go to jail. They're using torture. After you read this letter, destroy it and don't mention it to anyone." I never found out who had sent that letter.

"Count me in," I told Aziz.

We called ourselves the Afghan Refugee Aid Committee—ARAC. There were eight of us at the outset. We pooled our money to hire a lawyer and got ourselves incorporated as a nonprofit organization. We opened a bank account. I wrote some fund-raising letters, designed stationery, created leaflets.

We didn't raise much money, just a few donations from rich people whom I knew through the Asia Foundation, as well as a smattering of cash Aziz managed to squeeze out of other Afghans. But man, it felt good to use my crude publishing skills and American savvy to help Afghans! It helped alleviate the guilt I felt over being safe and sound in America.

And it gave me a vehicle for spending time with my Afghan pals. We had so much emotion to share about the old country, anger mostly, and anxiety, and sadness. We watched the news and moaned about events, drank beer and listened to tapes of Ahmad Zahir, the Elvis Presley of Afghanistan. I formed a close attachment to Akbar and Asghar Nowroz, whose names meant "big" and "little," although they were pretty much the same size, actually—in fact, they were fraternal twins. I made friends with Zalmay Shaghassi, a cheerful man whose manners were so smooth, they falsely made him seem false. I got to know Salik and Wafi and several others. Often the guys would spout poetry spontaneously; they all seemed to know hundreds of couplets by heart, and it didn't matter that I couldn't keep up. I can still close my eyes and see Akbar delivering a free-verse poem in Farsi with melancholy passion: "In this dark night ... crickets are lamenting. 'Oh moon! Oh, great moon ...' "

But soon trouble arose. It turned out we were not the only committee raising funds for Afghan refugees. Another group had formed, and they were twice our size! They demanded that we fold our operations and join them. Aziz and Zalmay stoutly warned them to shut down *their* committee and join us!

"Why can't we both exist?" I asked.

"We cannot both represent the Afghan community! We'll recruit new members. Let them see our strength."

Aziz dragged two recruits to our next meeting, but they immediately raised complaints. Why had we formed the committee without them? "Now all the good ministries are gone," they bellyached.

"Ministries?" I said.

It turned out they had examined our articles of incorporation, in which, conforming to legal necessity, we had listed some of ourselves as officers. They saw that Aziz had "appointed himself" president. My title of vice president translated to them as prime minister. And they correlated treasurer and secretary to Minister of Finance and Minister of Foreign Affairs.

I pleaded that we were not setting up a government in exile to replace the puppet government the Soviets had installed in Kabul: We were just trying to raise some money for refugees. But my own ARAC compatriots acted shamefaced and evasive, and I could see that the charges of personal ambition and nepotism had struck home. To placate the new guys, we offered them two plum portfolios, the Ministry of Interior and the Ministry of Defense, which they grabbed.

But how will we reward further recruits? I wondered.

Will we not run out of government posts? Are we lunatics? Just how many people are we competing for?

"At least thirty," I was told.

"Wow! You mean there are thirty Afghans here besides us? Who are they all?"

"Not thirty Afghans! Thirty Afghan *families*!"

One day, I got a call from a stranger who was concerned about the growing tension between our two committees. "We are inviting all the major Afghan leaders of the Bay Area to sit down together and achieve unity. Will you honor us?"

I had to laugh. "Me? An Afghan leader? You must be mixing me up with someone else. I haven't seen Afghanistan in seventeen years!"

He scoffed at my modesty. "You are an Ansary!"

At the Unity Council, I discovered that the older brother of our own Zalmay Shaghassi headed the other group. This struggle for legitimacy really came down to a rivalry between siblings.

Eventually, we did combine our two committees, but only because of an outside threat. *Another* committee was forming among the Afghans of Fremont, a suburb south of Oakland, and it was bigger than both of us—sixty families! As the Afghan proverb says, "Me against my brother, me and my brother against our cousins; we and our cousins against invaders."

And who knew but that even bigger groups might not

form? The community was growing as the war in Afghanistan blazed and spread. Already some half a million refugees were camped along the Pakistan-Afghanistan border. Virtually all of them came from rural villages, and nearly all were women and children; their men, the so-called mujahideen, or "holy warriors," were inside the country, fighting. Around the world in that era, war was driving whole families from their homes, but in Afghanistan, the refugee crisis had a terrible added dimension. Because only the women and children of each family were escaping to Pakistan, the war was fracturing families on a massive scale: Children were growing up without fathers. Their mothers, village women inculcated from infancy to feel shame when seen by strangers, now had to live in massive tent cities, without the protection of compound walls, exposed to just any passerby. Boys grew up in the shadow of what they must have felt to be their mothers' violation and shame. This was the unwholesome soil in which the Taliban eventually sprouted.

The refugees who made it to the United States came as whole families, but they were mostly urban Afghans from the upper bureaucratic class, the country's Westernized veneer. And they brought with them chilling tales. A schoolgirl named Na'eed told me about the day she and her classmates had demonstrated against the Soviets. They were marching in the streets, shouting, *"Allah-u-Akbar!"* ("God is great!"), when the Communist government sent jets to strafe them. Bullets felled the girl marching next to

Na'eed, and the flag she had been carrying fell from her hands, but Na'eed snatched it up and kept going. Here in America, her story got out to the media, and she was briefly canonized as the "Afghan Joan of Arc." She even got a photo op with President Reagan.

Then there was Siddiq, who had lived behind the notorious Pul-i-Khumri prison and could never get a good night's sleep, he said, because of the executions. These took place between midnight and dawn—not in rapid succession, but intermittently, so that it got on your nerves: Bang, someone died. Silence. You waited. Bang. Someone else died. Interval. Bang. You didn't know who was being killed or why, only that it was happening every night.

An older woman (one of Aziz's relatives, I think) told me that the Communists routinely extracted information from political activists by threatening to bury one of their relatives alive before their eyes. They made the threat credible by carrying through on it from time to time, and then setting the shocked witnesses free to spread their tales. "They say the soil seems to keep moving for hours," she reported. Fact or rumor? I don't know. But imagine how stories like that affected Afghans who had loved ones in that country; think of that phrase—"the soil seems to keep moving for hours."

Just as the committee struggles were peaking, Aziz called me. He had exciting news. "Subghatullah Mujadeddi is in

Florida. We can bring him here if we pay for his hotel and his airfare."

Subghatullah Mujadeddi: rebel warrior. His credentials came from having protested Soviet influence in Kabul twenty years before there *was* any. He'd even done prison time in the 1950s, Aziz told me, for demonstrating too loudly against a state visit by Khrushchev. Now, he led one of the seven main rebel parties based in Pakistan.

His last name suggested to me that he and Aziz were related in some way. I felt qualms. "Aziz, we're supposed to use our money to help refugees, not rebel leaders." Or our own relatives, I thought.

"But we use our money to make pamphlets! To host dinners!"

"That's called fund-raising."

"*This* will be fund-raising! He comes with his robe stained in the blood of martyrs. Who will not flock to see him?"

He had a point. A speech by a rebel warrior straight from the smoking battlefields of Afghanistan—by God, what a fund-raising opportunity! The more I thought about it, the more Aziz's excitement infected me.

So we rented California Hall, which seats hundreds of people. Akbar and I designed and printed leaflets and posters, and we went around on weekends stapling them to telephone poles and posting them in Laundromats. We bought round-trip plane tickets for the rebel leader and two of his aides. It cost more than we had in our ARAC account. No matter. We scraped up the difference from our own pockets. Zalmay filched money out of a family fund earmarked for rescuing more of his relatives from Afghanistan.

When the day came, a bunch of us went to the airport to meet the man. A good-sized crowd of Afghans had already gathered at the gate, rippling with excitement. He came off the plane wearing a long gray gabardine overcoat. His pinched little spectacles, his wispy white beard, and his puckered features gave him the look of a querulous, underpaid clerk. As he advanced through the sea of Afghans, everyone near him bowed at the waist, flexed their knees, and dropped their heads, assuming postures of deference. Subghatullah extended his hand, and anyone near enough grasped it and kissed it. He came past me, and what could I do? Though it felt awkward and unnatural, I knelt like the others and kissed his hand.

Aziz and the boys drove him to the Ramada Inn while I went to California Hall and attended to last-minute arrangements, checking the sound system, adjusting the lights, putting out literature, setting up the sidewalk sandwich board that announced AFGHAN REBEL LEADER TONIGHT! $10 (SLIDING SCALE).

I was hoping the hall would be big enough. Aziz told me busloads of Afghans were on their way up from Los Angeles, and the Afghan community in the Bay Area certainly numbered in the hundreds now, counting the Fremont souls!

But half an hour before the great man arrived, a number of Afghans came to me with worried faces. "On the door"—they fussed anxiously—"it says ten dollars?"

I gulped. "Is it too much?"

"Are you crazy? It is too little! You're telling the world our leader is worth ten dollars. It's humiliating! It's an insult to our dignity as Afghans!"

I felt my stomach clenching. "How much should we be charging?"

"*Charging?* What kind of host charges his guests? We can't charge money! We must welcome the multitudes, and when they leave, it should be *us* giving *them* gifts!"

I dismissed this point of view, but more Afghans came to me with the same complaint. Finally, my fellow ARAC members bowed to the majority, outvoted me, and scratched the charge. Our fund-raising event had turned into an example of free speech.

The hour was getting late, and the hall still looked pretty empty. "Where are the hordes of Afghans from Los Angeles? Shouldn't they be here by now?" I asked

"Oh, they're not coming," one of the twins told me diffidently. "We offended them."

"How on earth?"

"We invited Subghatullah without consulting them. They wanted to cohost his speech."

"What about the hordes of Bay Area Afghans?"

"Well, the Fremont Afghans are boycotting the speech."

"Boycotting! Why?"

So they explained it to me. To the Fremont Afghans,

this looked like a naked power grab: one member of the Mujadeddi family presenting another Mujadeddi to the American public, as if no one was fighting the Soviets except the Mujaddedis!

"So no Afghans are coming? And we're not charging money?"

"Never mind. It's better that Afghans don't take up seats. We want to save room for Americans. They're the ones we're trying to reach."

The first Americans to arrive were two men in bulky olive aviator jackets and berets. I recognized the type: hard-core lefties. In fact, they belonged to the Revolutionary Communist party, a tiny cadre of Marxist bullies who hung around the Twenty-fourth Street BART station, preaching Marxism through static-jangled bullhorns at uncaring crowds of rush-hour commuters. They found seats just behind me, and I heard them plotting how to ambush Mujadeddi with tough questions.

"If he mentions the third five-year plan, let's bring up the 1978 grain output from the Lenin Cooperative Farm. Ha! And then let's hit him with Comrade Dobransky's statement about the global solidarity of the working class! Ha-ha!" Stuff like that.

My mood sank. Since we weren't charging for seats, we were praying for donors. But if the few Americans who came were lefties bent on disruption . . .

Finally, Subghatullah arrived, surrounded by a constellation of reverent Mujadeddis and friends of Mujadeddis. He mounted the stage and sat on the rickety chair under the spotlight, blinking and peering into the crowd. The mike was set too high, so one of our committee people hurried onstage to pull it down. I could hear the RCP duo behind me, muttering, scribbling, plotting.

Then Subghatullah began to speak. That high-pitched, hectoring voice could scarcely be imagined inspiring warriors to go into battle. He gave a short speech. A very short speech. Well, to be blunt, it was extremely short. It lasted less than a minute, I think. Essentially, he said, "The Russians are your enemy. The Russians are my enemy. You Americans want to kill Russians. I *kill* Russians. Give me money and weapons, so I can kill more Russians. Thank you. Any questions?"

Behind me, the muttering and scribbling stopped. Here, finally, was an upside to our fund-raiser: Mujadeddi had coldcocked the RCP men. They had no idea how to deploy their intellectual artillery against this. No one asked any questions. Our event was over. We'd spent a thousand dollars, mostly out of pocket, borrowed in part from the Shaghassi Family Refugee Fund, and had nothing to show for it. Aziz accompanied me out the door. "Well!" He beamed. "That went very well, eh?"

Aziz was going to the Ramada Inn now because the rebel leader had agreed to meet with anyone who wanted to pay court. I was depressed, but I tagged along. To my surprise, his hotel room was already so jammed, the crowd bulged into the hall. Already he had a bigger audience here than he'd had for his speech. And as some people left, more kept arriving. In the course of the evening, I'd estimate that two hundred people filtered through.

I watched him work the crowd, and my whole impression of the man changed. During his speech, he had looked like such a small man on such a big stage. Here in the hotel room, what struck me was the sheer size of him. And today, I have no idea if he is actually big, small, or in between. It's not that he suddenly looked like a warrior. But the very traits that had diminished him in the American setting seemed to magnify him here. On that stage, he had looked like a clerk; here, like a cleric. There, pinched and querulous; here, studious and careworn. As he interacted with the Afghans, he emanated crackling intensity. His attention and presence never flagged or broke, and every interaction seemed intensely personal. "Oh, you're so-and-so? What ever happened to your uncle's goat, the one that kept damaging his hollyhocks?" He always had a name or two and some personal anecdote or reference to show that he wasn't just faking it. Sometimes he had to ask a few questions to establish the connection: "Your father is Abdul Farouk . . . ? Ah, in the Ministry of . . . ? Oh. Any relationship to General Nur Ali Khan? Why, I know him well!" Every person he spoke to ended up feeling known and important.

I was hoping he wouldn't notice me. I hated to disrupt his well-oiled social machinery. What could he possibly know about me? And if he knew anything, what could this conservative cleric bestow on me, a secularized, beer-

swilling sinner, except disapproval? Already, defensive, in-
dignant thoughts were zipping through my brain. Well,
hoity-toit to you, too, Mr. Mullah. Where do you come off
judging me? I have my principles, so you can just get your
sharia out of my face, thank you. . . .

Then his gaze settled upon me. Someone murmured
my name to him, and, amazingly, his face lit up with gen-
uine pleasure. "Wah! The son of Mir Amanuddin Ansary!
Ah, your father and I have shared many a good laugh. He
has a wonderful sense of humor. Some of his poems, you
know, are . . . quite ribald." His eyes twinkled in fond memory. Evidently, ribald was okay with him. I liked that.

His attention moved on, but he left me smiling. Hey,
this wasn't the rigid, sanctimonious stick I'd expected, but
a regular guy, pretty decent fellow really. How interesting
that my father made him laugh—with ribald jokes no less.
That was Daddy all right. And my heart glowed with affection for my warm and humorous father.

After a while, I realized he had worked me just as ex-
pertly as he had the others, but I didn't mind. I remained
impressed. In a flash, he had identified my family, scoped
me out, figured out how to disarm my suspicions, and
made our connection personal, with subtlety and grace.
Also, clearly, he really did know my father. Over the next
few hours, I saw him do the same thing flawlessly with at
least a hundred more people.

He answered questions, too. One American had somehow found his way into the hotel room that night, a big
gangly geek of a man called Weidenweber. He could tell

Mujadeddi was a religious figure, but he misinterpreted what that meant and asked the dumbest-possible question: "Sir, do you believe in magic? Is telepathy possible?"

Mujadeddi gave the question due consideration and a wry answer. "Magic is what we call any outcome whose technique is unknown to us. At one time, if you could talk in your own voice with someone hundreds of miles away, it would have been called magic. But now we call it the telephone. So yes, I think telepathy is possible; anything is possible, God willing, if the technique for it is discovered."

After the Communists fell, in 1992, Subghatullah Mujadeddi was the first rebel leader to serve as president of Afghanistan, but he lasted only a year or so. The political skills that got him there couldn't keep him there. He failed, I think, for the same reasons that our San Francisco committees failed. No one in Kabul cared about governing as a goal of government, just as no one in ARAC cared about fund-raising as a goal of a fund-raising committee. What people really cared about was who would bow to whom.

After that night, I receded from the committee. I lost faith in my ability to work on any project with other Afghans. They operated by rules I could not decipher. But the others receded, too, as their private lives rose around them like floodwater. Their families were coming, and they couldn't spare time or energy for refugees in Pakistan. They had refugees of their own to worry about, right here in the United States: parents, siblings, cousins. . . .

Aziz took the hardest hits of us all. As his relatives piled up on his shoulders in growing numbers, he tried so desperately to save everyone and worried so fretfully that he might save no one. He kept borrowing from his American wife's family to get his own people out. Finally, he buckled under the weight of his life and his sorrow for all Afghanistan, a burden he just didn't know how to put down, even for an instant.

Yet even as his life was going to pieces, his artistic urges were overflowing their banks, and he started transforming everything he owned or touched into art. He covered his tables and chairs with designs. He painted his walls and even his floor. He filled his car with objets d'art made from common items that he'd altered. Eventually, his beautiful American wife divorced him and he went crazy, became homeless, and died relatively young.

Meanwhile, my own family was trickling out of Afghanistan, too. They accumulated mostly in Portland, Denver, and Washington, D.C. My cousin Farid and his wife, Saman, settled in Virginia. They had been living with my father just before their escape. Farid told me that when they left Kabul, they had begged my father to come along, but he had refused.

"I'm old," he sighed. "What would I do in the West? I want to die in Afghanistan, so that I can be buried in the village."

And in 1982, his wish came true.

MY FATHER'S MASTERPIECE

I SAW MY FATHER ONLY twice after he moved back to Afghanistan, each time for only a couple of days. In 1970, the government sent him to the United States on business, and he eked out a side trip to Portland. When I ran to greet him as he got off the plane, he saw a wild-eyed, longhaired hippie and flinched in preparation for a mugging. After he recognized me, we were both embarrassed.

In 1977, he came to the United States for my sister's wedding, and afterward he visited with me in San Francisco. I had just moved to town and was living in temporary quarters, a sort of boardinghouse, where I had one room and limited access to a kitchen. I was doing better than my circumstances suggested, but my father couldn't see it. The sons of his expatriate friends in Washington, D.C., were all engineers and doctors now.

This was to be the last time I would see my father, but I

didn't know it: The young never know about last times. We were both longing to connect, however. And since we both loved words, we tried to do it through our writing.

I read to him from a surrealistic novel I had written in college, *Alice in Wonderbread and Several Dwarves*. He tried so hard to listen appreciatively, but his eyes kept glazing over. Oh, he did sit up once and look alert, and I thought, Wow, I got through to him. I wonder with what. But it turned out he was only looking past my shoulder at my bookshelves, where one book out of the hundreds had caught his eye: *Afghanistan*, by Louis Dupree.

Then he tried to read me a long narrative poem in Farsi that he had sent me several times. I guess he considered it his masterpiece. I knew it was funny, because he kept grinning, but that's about all I caught. Once in a while, he stopped to check that I understood some bit of tough vocabulary. "Do you know what *adeeli* means?"

"No."

"It means 'the equal of.' " And then he'd rush on, and I didn't have the heart to tell him, Daddy, I didn't understand a single word before or after *adeeli*, either!

When he left, he gave me his handwritten copy of that poem, hoping I would read it on my own and appreciate it someday, but I knew the chances were slim, given his bad handwriting and my fading Farsi.

I thought about that poem when he died, five years later. My mother broke the news. She called, and her voice was strange; she blurted it out before I could start on any inappropriate chitchat. "Daddy died."

When I heard that news, I felt . . . nothing. A curious ringing hollowness. He was gone from the world, and what did that change? I looked for the gap it would leave in my days but saw none. He'd been missing from my life since his return to Kabul in 1966, not counting those two brief visits. Otherwise, our only contact had been through letters. And since the Soviet invasion, his voice hadn't really been in his letters.

But I thought I should feel something, and then I did: I felt guilty that I didn't feel something. My mother sounded lost. I think she was going through an atheist's embarrassment about death. No matter what your religious beliefs may or may not be, death is big, and you feel it deserves—demands—a sacramental response. But what sacrament is available to an atheist?

Or perhaps the atheist's problem is more practical. Maybe everyone needs time to formulate emotions appropriate to the sudden news of death, but this is where organized religion takes over, for most people. The social apparatus swings into action, and you go through the motions, behind which, your feelings have time to mature. But we had no church, my mother and I, so my father's death left us swinging in our secular breeze.

It was my uncle who sent the news, in two letters to Rebecca, then a college professor in Pittsburgh. In typical Afghan fashion, he started with a preliminary letter to soften the blow, a false report that my father was merely ill.

A week or two later, he sent the follow-up letter, breaking the real news, that my father had died. The letters traveled at different speeds, however, so we got the news of his death first, and then, some weeks later, the report of his "illness."

He was sixty-two when he died. He had a heart attack. They took him to the hospital, but that may have killed him, medical facilities being what they were in Afghanistan. In the United States, I'm told, he probably would have survived that heart attack and might still be alive today. But then again, who knows.

The D.C. cousins sponsored a memorial service at the mosque, but I didn't have the money to fly there on such short notice, and besides, I didn't feel the mosque would help me deal with the death of this stranger who was my father.

Then my cousin Mazar called from Portland. He was almost exactly my age, and, along with Aziz and Najib, part of my core play group during my childhood in Old Kabul. Mazar invited me to come up to Portland for a day or two to mourn with his branch of the Ansarys informally. Grateful, I said yes.

I didn't pack much, just a change of clothes and that handwritten poem of my father's, the one I couldn't read. I wasn't going to be gone longer than the weekend. I felt some trepidation. I didn't want the Portland cousins to probe my feelings. I didn't want them to know what strangers my father and I had been. That fact felt shameful. I should have been there, I was thinking. I should never have left Afghanistan the way I did. When your mother and father live on opposite sides of the globe, you have to choose one or the other; one of them had to be hurt, but that didn't lessen the injury I'd done my father. I had robbed him of the one thing an Afghan man values most—his eldest son.

Most of the Portland cousins were the progeny of my prolific eldest uncle, the grim-faced general. He was long dead, but his redoubtable wife, Mahgul, had survived and was presiding. Her children had come to the States one by one. As each one arrived, he got a job and saved money until he could bring another one over—who then got a job, and they both saved money until, together, they could bring another one over. All of her children got to the United States eventually, and then they brought Mahgul over, too. They lived in one large house in northeast Portland, furnished in the spare Afghan manner, mostly bare of furniture, no adornment on the clean white walls except quotations from the Koran rendered in fine gilt-edged calligraphy.

The cousins read a little Koran while I listened, but mostly we talked about my father. And I discovered that I did remember a few stories: how he used to come home from work at 3 p.m. in Lashkargah and get straight into his pajamas, for example, because he suffered from insomnia. If he felt even a tremor of drowsiness at the office, he hurried home in great excitement, hoping that this time he would fall asleep. He never succeeded, of course. He claimed he hadn't slept in twenty years.

And I remembered how my father got interested in cartooning for a month or so. He came home one day with a doodle that made us laugh. Next day, two doodles that made us laugh, then ten. He worked up like that till he was pouring out drawings, filling notebooks, covering envelopes. Finally one day, he brought home a fully rendered, realistic portrait of someone—and that ended it. He stopped drawing and never picked up a drawing pencil again.

The longer I talked, the more stories I discovered. It turned out that my father was not such a stranger to me after all. His personality lay buried in mine. I really did know the man. There was the time he took me to the Watermelon Festival, the time he took me across the Desert of Death to the alabaster mines, those quiet moments during Ramadan when I woke up with him to have bread and tea before dawn. He told me then about *laila t'ul qadr,* the night when all of creation bows down to God and something wonderful happens to you if you witness it, but you never do, because you just can't stay awake, and I'd try so hard to stay awake.

And my cousins told their stories, of which they had more than I did, because they had known him better, or at least later. Through their eyes, I saw a father I had never known. To them, he had his own archetypal place among the five brothers. Just as Khan Kaka was the peppery intellectual, and Jan Agha the fierce military man, my father was the puckish prankster, the jokester, the life of every party. Little kids could be sure of getting money from him at *eid*, the major Muslim holiday. The older boys knew he'd pull them aside at parties and give them surreptitious sips of his homemade strawberry wine. When the teenagers needed to talk to some adult, they went to my father, because he was the approachable one, the beloved uncle. Gosh, it made me wish *I'd* been one of his nephews.

Although he was vice rector of Kabul University, a big, solemn job, he stayed on the edge of trouble with his incorrigible joking. He rewrote patriotic, sentimental odes that were recited at ceremonial occasions, poems that pompously praised Afghanistan, praised Kabul, the flag, the martyrs of Maiwand. By changing words here and there, sometimes just letters, he rendered them absurd, even scatological. What a naughty guy. "Oh Kabul! Your skirts are mountains splattered with flowers" became "Oh Kabul! Your skirts are mountains splattered with shit!"

Pashto was the language of the ruling clan and the official language of Afghanistan, and no one was allowed to make fun of it or insult it. My father infuriated the authorities by going the other way. He championed Pashto too much, loudly proclaiming it "the mother of all the languages." He drew up lexicons of words in Pashto and other languages that sounded similar, and drew forced etymological connections. The name Mexico, he claimed, derived from the Pashto phrase *"Maka sikaway."* Pashtuns, he explained, had discovered Mexico but didn't like it, and when they came home, they told their friends, *"Maka sikaway,"* which means "What are you doing? Don't do that." He also lamented that foreign words had crept into common usage, spoiling the purity of our Afghan tongue—why use an English word like *motor* for *car*? Why not use a good Pashtu word?—and he offered his suggestion, a phrase in Pashto that means "donkeys with wheels."

His interest in humor extended to scholarship. Everywhere he went in Afghanistan, he collected jokes. He'd compiled about a thousand of them in a book, jokes from every part of the country. What a resource that vanished document would have been for ethnographers.

On my way home from that short visit, an amazing thing happened to me. I took out that handwritten copy of my father's poem on the plane and discovered I could read it now. Of course, this was probably because I had been spending so much time with Afghans since I'd last seen him, but it felt like a miracle all the same. Oh, it wasn't like reading a printed text in English, but I looked at that first line—*"K'noon suhbat az mawr-geeree shinow"*—and I could see what it meant and how the meaning was constructed: "Now hear some conversation about catching snakes." And the next line: *"Ugar bikhradi, andur een rah marow."* Yes, that was intelligible, too. "If you are wise, do not go down this path."

A way to translate the first two lines into a rhyming couplet popped into my head: "Now listen to advice about the snake-charming art./That's a path you will not follow if you're smart." Not great, but hey, it rhymes and does convey the literal meaning of the lines. I got to wondering if I could translate more couplets. And in the years that followed, I translated them all. I translated the whole poem three times, created three different versions, because I learned that every line could be translated many ways. "Let us now discuss the snake-handling vocation. / If you're sensible, you know, you'll shun that occupation." See what I mean?

Translating my father's poem became my way of getting to know his mind. Too bad I started after he was dead. But you know what? A relationship doesn't end with death. It doesn't even stop growing. I have discovered that my father's thoughts and works and spirit permeate my life. I continue to learn more about him as I ponder his narrative and meet the people who knew him.

I called my mother after I got back from Portland to tell her what had happened and to hear about the service in the mosque. She told me two hundred people had attended, my father being so well known and liked, and the mullah's chanting of the Koran had moved her deeply. She told me that the service made her think of Daddy, and what he'd meant to her. They had lived apart all those years, but in the end, he was the man in her life; there was no other. And when she thought back over it all, she saw that marrying him and going to Afghanistan for those twenty years was her life's great adventure, the core episode that gave her narrative its meaning.

"I know," I said. "When he died, a thought went through my mind, you know, like, What did he ever do for me? He left me; I made my way alone, no help from him. But in Portland, I realized that he gave me quite a lot, actually. He gave me his spirit, and he gave me . . ."

I saw what word was coming, and I had to pause for the swell of emotion. How could I have failed to notice this gift? Not that I discount my mother—she gave it to me, too. It takes two to make one; that's the point of the universe. Come together.

"He gave me life."

And then the tears. We both wanted to cry, and we did cry at last. I guess it was partly for my father, that he'd ended his journey, poor fellow: For better or for worse, his arc was complete. But I wept for myself, too, for the dawning knowledge that life is not an entitlement, but a gift.

When I think of the soul, I don't go with the "wine in a bottle" metaphor. I think of my own soul like light from a candle. It begins in me but is not contained in me. It surrounds me, thinning out as it radiates into the universe. It's in my relationships, in the traces I leave as I move through the world, in the people I love and those who love me. It's in the hatreds that enmesh me, too. When I think of the soul that way, I can see that it doesn't end with death, since we're all living in one another's light. I think about my father and how he's grown for me since he died, and how he keeps on growing, and I know he isn't dead as long as he lives in me and in his friends and in what he added to and subtracted from the world. On that score, I think he did okay. I only hope I can do as well.

THE ART OF LOSING

RIAZ AND I can have a friendly conversation now if we choose our topics carefully. But it's not like it used to be when we were growing up. Everything changed one night after our father died. I know about that night chiefly from the archives; I have historical evidence for it: a diary entry that reads "Big fight with Riaz." and a bunch of letters that passed between us in the aftermath— they're still in my files and chronicle what was said. But when I scan my memory bank for the actual details, I find only tatters and fragments, like recollections from a night of ruinous drinking. We were on the phone with each other. Why? I don't remember. Did we used to call each other back then, just to say hi? It's hard to believe. But damn, the love was there at one time, so long as certain conventions were maintained. I was big brother; he was little brother. I was teacher; he was learner. I was right; he was wrong. Those were my rules, the conditions of my love, though I didn't know it.

Riaz was responsible for getting me married. When I got back from Turkey, Debby and I moved into our own place and set up housekeeping. To me, that seemed like an end point. What else did we need? Marriage? Oh please. Marriage just wasn't done in the counterculture. If you love each other, why do you need that little piece of paper? Just ask Joni Mitchell or any other sixties relic. Even to mention it would have been in bad taste.

Then Riaz decided to get married. He had no particular woman in mind. I don't know what emotions drove his decision. They didn't include desire, apparently. Desire for whom? It was more that the scriptures said a Muslim should get married and raise a family, and so he set about those obligations like all the others in his usual earnest way.

He traveled around the United States, from one Muslim community to another, which he did anyway, with all his savings and spare time, because he saw himself as a missionary, not to unbelievers, but to Muslims. In each community, he conducted himself in scrupulous accordance with the rules and guidelines of Islam so that others might see how it was done and be inspired by his good example. You might say that being holier than thou was his vocation.

But now, as he toured Muslim communities, he asked

men if they knew of a suitable wife for him. If they did, a meeting was arranged. Riaz and the candidate got together and talked, with a male relative standing by as chaperone. Afterward, each made a decision, yes or no.

His quest amused me. No, *bemused* might be a better word. I still had a tolerant attitude then. Riaz had chosen a lifestyle very different from mine, but not, perhaps, more different than mine was from my parents' when I became a radical longhaired hippie. Some of my friends compared Riaz to a Hare Krishna and assured me he would grow out of this phase, but I knew Riaz was more like a Buddha than a Hare Krishna. There was nothing mindless or callow about his conversion.

Among Muslims, he was acquiring some stature for his uncompromising devotion and growing scholarship. A number of communities had invited him to act as their imam, their religious specialist. In his own circles, I'm sure he had charisma, even macho charisma. He was short and scrawny, and had just enough beard to amuse, but he radiated strength. Not the "I'll beat you up" kind, but the "You don't scare me" kind. You looked in this man's eyes, and you were looking at flint and steel. Riaz inherited his complexion from our mother, making him about as white as white guys get, but he lived in the angriest, most bombed-out black ghetto neighborhoods of Washington, D.C., because that's where the Muslims lived, and he walked those streets without fear. In his spare time, he ministered to Muslims in some of America's toughest prisons.

He drove a motorcycle—not to be macho, but to save

money: He couldn't afford a car. But still, when this slight figure in flowing white Muslim garb pulled up at some mosque on his Harley, fresh from converting murderers at the penitentiary, I have to suppose he swashed some buckle—in his quiet way.

He interviewed wife candidates for a year, but no one clicked. It struck me that I might help him. After all, some of the Afghans I knew had devout sisters or cousins. I called Debby at work one day to see what she thought of my finding Riaz a wife. A silence ensued. Then she burst forth: "You're so busy arranging your brother's life! Why don't you arrange your own life first!"

The words startled me. Was she talking about . . . ? What happened to property is theft, marriage is slavery? "You want to get married?" I stammered.

Debby claims she had no idea those words were going to come out of her mouth. She had not been thinking about marriage. But now that it was on the table, after due consideration, she admitted that yes, all in all, she'd rather be married than not.

And my attitude was: Either way. Whatever. Which being true, it struck me that getting married might be a hoot. The poet Gérard de Nerval used to walk a lobster on a leash down the Champs-Elysées—"to astound the bourgeoisie," he claimed. I saw getting married as just such a gesture, a lobster-on-a-leash with which to flabbergast my former hippie friends. We made a casual appointment to meet at City Hall, and I told my boss at Harcourt Brace, where I was then an editor, that I would need a couple of hours off on Friday.

"Why?" she said.

I shrugged. "I'm getting married."

She gave me a look. "Take the whole day."

And that's how Riaz nudged me into marriage.

Our casual ceremony before a tipsy judge segued into an elaborate dinner with close friends, which segued into more dinners with more friends, which faded into a honeymoon in the Yucatán. This was followed by a big reception at a country club in Washington, D.C., thrown by Debby's father, and then, back in San Francisco, by the biggest party we had ever thrown. It was at a rented place called the Farm, with the band from Debby's theater troupe, Make-a-Circus, providing the sound track (they were delighted to stretch beyond "Shave and a haircut, two bits").

My Afghan friends surprised me by renting a limousine to take us from our apartment to the party. They also set up all the rituals of an Afghan wedding for us—the wedding throne, the henna for the wedding guests' palms, the crumbled sweet bread, the embroidered blanket that was thrown over our heads and the mirror that was thrust under it, the mirror in which we were supposed to see each other for the first time. A little late for that in our case, since we had already been together two years, but it was fun.

And then, because Debby is Jewish, we danced the hora

and wrapped a wineglass in towels and crushed it underfoot and did other Jewish wedding rituals, and everybody loved all of it and we all got along. In short, our spur-of-the-moment courthouse wedding turned into a party that spanned the continent and two or maybe more cultures and lasted for a month.

I never did find Riaz a wife, but eventually he found his own, an African-American woman from New Jersey who had converted to Islam. We took different routes to marriage, but we both ended up with solid ones. He and Aisha got married in a room with a curtain down the middle of it. The men sat on one side, and they could see only Riaz up there on the stage; the women sat on the other side, and they could see only Aisha. Rebecca and my mother attended Riaz's wedding, but I wasn't invited. I guess it came sometime after that terrible night.

Ah yes, that night.

What triggered it was a set of pages Riaz sent me, photocopies from a book on Islam, written by his kind of Muslim, elaborating—with nuance and intelligence—a concept of Islam as both social project and spiritual experience. They explained that Islam speaks to the community with *sharia,* the law, and the soul with *salaat,* the prayer ritual: *sharia* and *salaat,* mirrors of each other, internal and external versions of the same "project." That word *project,* however, rang a bell for me. Social project. Spiritual project. What echo was I hearing? I dug through the notes from my trip to North Africa and Turkey, and there it was. Abdul Qayum, the Puerto Rican Muslim in the pin-striped suit, the enthusiast I met in Turkey—he had used this very language, had propounded these same ideas. Exactly these ideas. Either these were common coin in modern-day Islamic thought or Riaz and Abdul Qayum had been drinking from the same stream.

Not that I saw anything sinister in the water from this stream.

But then a new factor entered the equation.

Shortly after I read Riaz's document, I wandered into a San Francisco bookstore that specialized in "spiritual" books—pop Hinduism, astrology, Gurdjieff, and so on. But there, in one corner, I saw a display of books put out by the same London publisher that had issued the books Abdul Qayum had given me. I recognized them from their cover design first, and then by the publisher's name. I bought three of them.

The first two covered much the same ground as the pages Riaz had given me. The design of all three was so uniform, they looked like a series. One book set forth the function of the law. The second described the benefits of prayer.

The third one revealed the secret of history.

Let me see if I can get this across clearly. I don't have the books anymore. Sometimes a bad experience acts like a flashbulb, puts a harsh glare on a memory. But I don't think I'm falsifying or exaggerating. Here's the theory in a few broad strokes.

To the untutored eye, history looks like a wriggling snake pit full of disparate but interwoven dramas; the Romans battling the Parthians, Columbus discovering America, the Industrial Revolution, World War II, etc.

Bunk, said the third book. That's all a smoke screen for innocents. The real drama of history is a secret, simple struggle between God and Satan.

Satan's forces act through a hidden cabal of evil people who secretly control all of the world's governments. This cabal existed in ancient Egyptian times as a cult of priests called the Rosicrucians, headed by the pharaoh. The pyramid represents Satan's "social project": a top-down structure with a single, supreme false god at the pinpoint, directing an ever-broadening bureaucracy, which lords it over an even broader base of suffering masses. That's why the pharaoh, executive director of Satan's people on Earth, forced his slaves, Abraham's progeny, the People of the Book, to build pyramids. And that's also why virtually all ancient cultures built pyramids when they first launched into monumental architecture. Even in pharaonic times, the supreme leader kept watch over the masses through a network of spies, and therefore the central Rosicrucian symbol was a pyramid with an eye in the middle of it.

Now take a look at the U.S. dollar bill. There it is—the pyramid with the eye!

How did the Rosicrucians (aka Satan) come to control American currency? Ah, that takes us to the next diabolical link. The Rosicrucians, supposedly, disbanded their cult and reorganized as the Masons, another secret society.

Since then, all top rulers, all kings, emperors, presidents, and the like, have secretly been Masons. They carry out a pretense of fighting wars with one another, but only the regular people die in these wars, never the rulers. That's because all these Masons are secretly in cahoots, all busy carrying out their only actual project, on behalf of Satan, which is to subjugate believers to unbelievers and eliminate God's message from the Earth.

Now it gets weird. All right, it's been weird already, but now it gets scary. According to this book, the people who now call themselves Jews aren't really Jews. They're really a tribe from the Caucasus region, where they were known as the Khazars. And indeed, historically, there was a tribal empire by this name situated smack-dab between the Islamic and the orthodox Christian realms; the people of this tribe converted en masse to Judaism in the 1300s or so as a means of preserving the empire's independence in the face of its larger neighbors, but the Khazars, according to the third book, were actually invented by the Masons.

The theory maintains that the Masons infiltrated and subjugated the Khazars, converted them to Judaism by fiat, and sent them forth into the world, so as to replace the world's real Jews with these fake Jews.

And now you can see where this is going: It's about Israel.

As I reckon it, Muslims and Jews have no serious quarrel on theological grounds. Original Islam saw Muslims, Jews, and Christians as cousins nourished by a single message. Islam accepts Christ, David, Moses, and all the

Judaic prophets and patriarchs as "messengers." In light of this tenet, how can Muslims deny Jewish claims to a homeland in Palestine?

The third book was offering a way. Disconnect Jews from Judaism, that's how. The real Jews, it was preaching, the ones respected by Muhammad, were gone. Israel was peopled by fake Jews, and therefore could be regarded without heresy as Satan's beachhead in the Muslim world, the front line in a vast secret war between believers and unbelievers.

It sounds like something only a few scattered loonies could find convincing, right? Well, I don't know. What alarmed me was its internal coherence. Every plank supported every other plank. Once you're inside such a house, you can never get another message from the outside world. The windows are all mirrors, and the house can reshape every incoming piece of information into another beam in its own framework. New information can only confirm the theory, never disprove it. "Look what those infidels are up to now! Didn't I tell you they were tricky?" Such thinking dissolves a lot of arguments. It wasn't the first time I had noticed an intellectual structure of this type. It seems to me that every cult relies on some version of it. Jim Jones used it to build Jonestown. Therapy cults do something like this by reducing every argument, every idea, to a symptom. Cults have used these mechanisms to hijack Marxism and Christianity and other broad belief systems.

I began to worry that Riaz believed this stuff. The pages he had sent me matched the content of those first two books from the London group. They said nothing about a secret meaning to history, but then, he didn't send me the whole book. What was in the pages he didn't offer me?

I don't remember how our phone conversation began or who called whom. I don't remember what was said exactly. I do remember pacing and trembling. I know I confronted him about the pamphlet. He didn't deny the idea of a war between believers and unbelievers.

"Everyone has to believe in God before the problems can be corrected. In that sense, yes, every conflict is about the realm of Islam versus the realm of chaos. Jihad is the cutting edge of that change."

I ferociously disputed the proposition that every conflict was about Islam. "South Africa!" I shouted. "Apartheid!"

"Apartheid cannot exist in Islam. If everyone follows the *sharia* willingly, there can be no injustice."

"*Willingly?* Any ideology works if everybody follows it *willingly!* That's the PROBLEM! Everyone isn't going to follow your Islam *willingly!* I won't. Start with me. I don't want to live in your perfect world. I hate your perfect world. I despise the idea of separating women and men the way you want to. That's my idea of a culture built on rape. *Willingly?* Stop lying to yourself, and admit you're talking about force."

I don't remember his answer. I wasn't listening. Later that night, I asked him what he was going to do when his jihad reached Washington. "Are you going to kill Mommy?"

He didn't deny it.

And then we got into Israel, and I proved to my own satisfaction that he was saying Israel had no right to exist.

"It doesn't," he said. "They took that land."

"So you want to erase Israel! What about Israelis? What about all those people? Kill them all, is that what you're saying?"

"They took the land," he muttered through clenched teeth.

"Goddamn it, Riaz! Debby's Jewish! My child can be considered Jewish. Do they have a right to exist? *Well, do they?*" I screamed.

"They took the land," he repeated stubbornly, unhappily.

I was raving that night, pushing him with extreme statements, trying to get him to say no, he would never do such a thing, that he had made a mistake; trying to get him to say that I was right and he was wrong after all! But he wouldn't say no. Maybe he didn't want to dignify my aggressive questions with answers. Maybe he refused to accept an obligation to justify his views to his big brother. I don't know. Months later, he sent me a handsome apology in a letter, allowing that he may have said or implied things he didn't mean. But the damage was done.

I don't know how the conversation ended. Eventually, it was over; that's all I know. And for the next few days, I couldn't see my feelings through the thick cloud cover of rage. And when that finally dissipated, I realized I felt sick. Not sore-throat sick, but nausea-sick, a stumbling-through-smelly-swamp-gas, worms-in-my-belly kind of sick. And only after that dissipated did I see the vast landscape over which I was flying: sadness, sadness as far as the eye could see.

I sat down then and wrote about the two of us killing the lamb that day in Maryland. Writing about it made me remember the younger Riaz, and how solicitous I used to feel toward him. It made me remember that rainy day in San Francisco when I dropped him off at the freeway entrance, a little boy who was set to hitchhike across the continent all by himself and then go off to Pakistan, all the way around the world. I remembered exactly how I had felt and what I had thought as I drove away that day: that he'd never come back. Yes, that's what had troubled my thoughts—I had worried that he'd never come back. And oh, how relieved and glad I was when I saw him coming back after all, coming down the ramp at the airport a year later wearing his Pakistani clothes, his skullcap, and his tight, diplomatic smile. Now it occurred to me that my happiness had been unwarranted. A sentence popped into my head, and I wrote it down as a last line for my story about killing the lamb. This was the sentence: "The little boy who walked away from me in the rain that day never did come back."

And seeing the sentence I had written, I burst out crying. And even now as I look at that sentence, I feel the tears. When Debby came home, my eyes were red, and she thought I had a cold. But then my little Jessamyn, my first daughter, that darling bulb of fresh life, just two years old at this point, wanted to show me her new cloth giraffe, so I stuffed my sorrow into a closet to deal with later, and started the rest of my life.

"The art of losing isn't hard to master," says Elizabeth Bishop in a famous poem, but I'm not so sure. The art of losing, I find, *is* kind of hard to master. Since that fight, Riaz has often used the word *brother* over the years, but never again in reference to me. Today, he has a hundred million brothers in the world, but I'm not one of them. Just this year, we crossed paths at my mother's house, and his ten-year-old son, whom I liked immediately and who took to me warmly, asked, "How did you meet my father? Were you friends?"

I pondered what had happened to Riaz when he returned from Pakistan. He brought back something he considered wonderful. He brought it back as any kid might bring a trophy home from school, expecting congratulations, praise, and love. But that's not what we gave him.

I considered how it must have hurt him when we all said, "Ooh, get that creepy thing out of here; you make my skin crawl." It must have hurt, but I didn't notice, because I was too busy being right, and to that extent, I guess I won: I *was* right. I still am.

HANGING ON

FOURTEEN YEARS PASSED, during which Afghanistan dropped out of my consciousness. That's my
quick impression. I sank into my American life: my
private life, my family, my career, my friends, my house,
and growing older.

But looking closer, I see that Afghanistan never vanished; it remained a shimmering thread in the embroidery
always. All through the late nineties, I was working on a
novel about Afghanistan. Before that, come to think of it, I
published a children's book about Afghanistan. Oh, and
before that, I made friends with macho journalists and ad-
venturers who traveled with the mujahideen and wrote
books about their exploits. I scoured their pictures, de-
voured their stories. And I renewed my friendship with my
cousin Mazar. I danced at his wedding. I wept over his
death.

And there were other Afghan weddings, and other deaths, too, because almost all of the Ansarys left Afghanistan and came to America. Maybe that's what gives me the impression that I lost track of Afghanistan. My Afghanistan came here.

But I always had a "one toe in and nine toes out" relationship with my clan. I remember the first time I met another Ansary in this country. He headed for Portland, thinking I was there. I was already gone, but he somehow found a job right away, so he settled there. When he came to see me, I drove him around San Francisco, showing him the sights. He was my age, although not particularly a close buddy in the old days. And he embarrassed me at once by hanging his head out the window and yelling at some women on the sidewalk, "Shake it, baby!" (He later confided to me that this was how men were supposed to act in America: He knew from careful observation.) Yet the sense of kinship that I felt with this man went right to my head like strong drink. It didn't have to do with both of us being Afghans. It had to do with Ansary-ness.

Once enough Ansarys had collected here, I sometimes found myself in real Ansary family gatherings, and it always gave me a timeless feeling, as if the purpose of all effort was to get to this place: hanging around with a bunch of Ansarys. It was a taste of permanence, however fleeting, because I knew the great Ansary self would be there no matter what particular Ansarys came or went.

Yet meshing with the clan was often like changing gears without a clutch. I remember saying to my cousin Zahir early on, "Come over. When are you free? Let's make a date." And he said, "Oh no, I'll never set a date. I'll drop in when you least expect it. I'll just happen to be in your neighborhood one day; I'll call you from a roadside pay phone and be on your doorstep five minutes later."

He was being courteous. I found it exasperating.

I think all of us Afghans tried at first to establish here a sense of those private family villages we grew up with, but in America, you can't keep out what's public. You watch TV, you go to work, you make friends there, you have no walls around your house, and you live next to strangers. When Afghans were first arriving in America, I often heard stories of grandmothers moving restlessly from household to household, city to city, coast to coast, unable to find contentment anywhere. I believe they were looking for the heart of the clan, the household so deeply private that they could be surrounded only by their own, so central that they could taste all the currents of clan life without moving from one house. They were looking for a mythical place that didn't exist, that couldn't exist, in America.

In the early days, I had to be careful about calling my cousins when I went through their towns, because they would pull me in, pin me to the mat, and smother me in so much hospitality, I felt guilty. I felt guilty because I could never reciprocate. True Afghan hospitality doesn't mesh too well with a typical American lifestyle.

Debby and I maintain a nuclear household, we both work, we have dozens of close friends to whom we're related by interests, not blood, and our calendar is full of public obligations such as parent-teacher conferences and neighborhood action meetings. My daughter Jessamyn was born in 1983, my daughter Elina in 1991. Being there for the girls, and for Debby, being a good citizen, succeeding in my work, and maybe securing the affection of my friends—these are my preoccupations as an American.

Being a good host, being a good guest, proving one's generosity, and putting kinship above all—these are the central preoccupations of an Afghan. And I think I know where the values come from. Before technology, in our hard, dry land, we lived on the edge. We didn't have the luxury of considering each individual as a sovereign state and every social relationship as voluntary. We couldn't think in terms of leveling the playing field and giving everyone an equal chance in the competition of all against all—a fundamental premise of democracy in a modern Western state. Living like that could have killed us.

Instead, we developed a culture that said, No one is ever on their own. Everyone belongs to a big group. The prosperity and survival of the group comes first. And no, everyone is not equal. Some are patriachs, and some are poor relations; that's life. But generosity is the value that makes it all work.

In the private universe of the extended-extended-extended family, nothing counts like prestige, and nothing confers prestige like largesse. Americans seem to think of Afghans as bearded gunmen who live for war, but actually, for Afghans, generosity far outweighs military prowess. And having more than the other guy is almost worse than having nothing. If you want to derive happiness from wealth, you have to play the expansive host and feed the multitudes. Every important occasion demands an extravagant display. A marriage can break a family, financially. So can the death of an important man, for his survivors. Even good fortune is linked to generosity rituals. If something good happens to you, it's an opportunity to throw a public feast—to give *khairat*.

When Afghans first started moving to the United States in significant numbers, they came clothed in the raiment of the old customs. They married their own, and cousins competed to outhost one another. They tried to hold on to everything, because they thought they were going back. But the customs softened over time. People had to fit into the clockwork schedules of America, and eventually they did. The grandmothers settled. A few people even married out of the clan. A few, a very few, even married Americans. Just a couple of years ago, I noticed how much easier it was to interact with other Ansarys. It was not anything I had learned; it was they who were changing, letting go of habits brought over from the lost world, becoming Americans.

Talk of going home, so common at first, faded as the news from Afghanistan did what it has done throughout my adult life: got worse. In 1992, the Communist government collapsed and the rebel warriors marched into Kabul, and there was cautious celebration among Afghans. Was it time? Could the grandmothers start packing at last?

No way. Now the news turned really horrific. The various rebel factions spread through Kabul and took over separate neighborhoods. Within two days, the gunfire started sounding. A power-sharing agreement among the factions tattered like wet toilet paper. The two most powerful parties took the two most powerful posts. Burhanuddin Rabanni, the head of one group, got the presidency. Gulbuddin Hikmatyar, head of the other group—a ruthless fundamentalist extremist—became prime minister.

"President" Rabanni moved into headquarters downtown. "Prime Minister" Hikmatyar set up his artillery on the hills west of Kabul and began shelling the city. Once in a while, he called a brief truce and made his way downtown under heavy guard for a cabinet meeting. Such was the government of Afghanistan.

Kabul dissolved into fiefdoms ruled by ethnic gangs that called themselves political parties. To go from one neighborhood to another in those years, you needed an agreement between two warlords, as well as an armed escort. Casual pedestrians could not cross main streets, because stepping into the open could get you gunned down. If San Francisco were like that, I wouldn't be able to go to Safeway, because it would mean crossing Mission Street.

No, it still wasn't a good time to go back. Everyone put their plans on hold again. And then, as if from nowhere, the Taliban appeared. They drove the warlords out of Kabul, and the gang wars faded. Wherever they took over the countryside, the minor warlords succumbed to them, and the bandits fled. Some semblance of order emerged.

Frankly, I felt a tremor of hope, as did most Afghans. Oh, I dreaded the Taliban's conservative religiosity. They were not out to build a society I wanted to live in; but then, I wasn't planning to live in it, so they were not obligated to please me—or any of the exiles, much less foreigners. Those who had stayed and survived the war against the Soviets had gone through hell. Surely they had won the right to restore the world they had lost.

That's how it looked to me at first. The Taliban were trying to restore the lost world. Women wore *burqa*s in public? Well, they did when I was young. In the bazaars, you saw only men? That's how it was when I was young. Everybody prayed? Everybody fasted during Ramadan? All the men wore beards? Sounded familiar. It sounded like they were saying, Let's go back forty years and try again, this time without the West, without the Soviets, without any outside interference. Sure, it would be a heartbreaking shame for poor Afghanistan to have to start over, but restoring the lost world wouldn't be so bad if only there could be peace. And with stability, I felt sure, social change would come again.

Then the news began to trickle out—an item here, an item there. Women were forbidden to wear squeaky shoes. What did that have to do with the lost world? Windows were to be painted black, so no one could see a woman. Whoa! Guys! It was *never* like *that*! What about the women's opportunity to look out? The private realm was supposed to be a garden, not a prison.

Then, music was outlawed. Were they crazy? Afghans love music! What was next? Kite flying, ha-ha?

Yes. Kite flying *was* next. And then it got worse. Women

beaten. Women's hospitals shut down. Girls' schools closed. Widows pleading to be allowed out of the house—and not even to work, just to beg—but being driven back with sticks. How were they going to eat? Women without men, forced to stay indoors—this went beyond imprisonment. This was slow murder. These Taliban were out of control. Didn't they remember how it was?

It dawned on me that no, they didn't. The Taliban were, in fact, the boys who had grown up in the refugee camps in Pakistan. They had never tasted how it was. They knew nothing of the lost world except for scattered phrases they heard from their fathers and uncles, who came out of Afghanistan rarely, and then on stretchers, veins hanging from severed limbs, choking out the words "Son, always kill infidels; never let strangers see our women."

In the late eighties, I remember, I was looking at some photos my friend Bob Darr had taken in the Pakistan refugee camps, pictures of boys horsing around and mugging for the camera. They looked like boys anywhere, except that they all had machine guns. Bob remarked, "These boys have emotional problems."

"What?"

"These boys in the camps, they're carrying a lot of anger, and if you talk to them, you just feel there's something missing. They are going to cause problems someday."

His casual comment reminded me of an interview I had seen on TV some years earlier. "Would you like to go to America?" the interviewer asked a twelve-year-old boy from the Kandahar area.

The boy wasn't sure. "Do they have fighting there?"

"No, in America you can live in peace."

"Oh, then I don't want to go. Afghanistan is better. Here you can fight and fight, kill your enemies every day."

The Taliban were these boys grown to manhood. Expecting them to restore the lost world was like hoping for Charles Manson to resurrect the Summer of Love.

I had only one cousin left in Afghanistan, a woman named Zahida. Shortly after the Taliban took charge, she got a message out to me. My father's house was (amazingly) still intact, and someone wanted to buy it for a lot of money. She needed permission from me and my siblings to close the deal. Of course I said yes, knowing she could use that money to escape. Rebecca and I signed off on it at once, but Riaz balked. He worried that squatters holed up in the old house would be displaced by the sale. So the opportunity expired. Zahida remained in Kabul.

But it left me wondering: How could a property in Kabul fetch thirty thousand dollars? How on earth could anyone in that bombed-out, wretched city pay that kind of money? I poked around and learned the answers from the latest refugees coming over. Rich Arabs and Pakistanis had flooded into the country in the wake of the Taliban. They were buying up Kabul, bidding against one another, driving the prices up. Afghans had been pushed to the sidelines in their own country, unless you counted the Taliban—who were Afghans genetically but had come from Pakistan physically.

In the north, the Taliban were driving Ahmed Shah Massoud, the last effective Afghan nationalist, steadily up into the most remote corner of the country. The Taliban had plenty of fresh weapons, you see—they attacked Kabul with seven hundred brand-new tanks. Massoud was down to the last rusty remnants of weaponry he'd gotten from the United States and, to a lesser extent, from France. No one cared about him anymore, now that Soviet communism had collapsed. He gave a speech in 1997, which I heard on the Afghan radio station in Fremont, warning frantically of new foreigners invading Afghanistan, Arabs and Pakistanis this time. He smuggled videotapes out to Afghans in the West, showing rural military camps crawling with these foreigners. As far as I know, none of these tapes were ever shown on television, because the war in Afghanistan had no audience. It was so eighties.

I found myself getting emotional about the country again. It may have started in 1999, when I stumbled across a Web site posted by Help the Afghan Children, a charity run by Afghans. The HTAC people had good connections inside the country. They went in with medicine and supplies; they came out with pictures and news.

And here is the news they brought. Afghanistan was full of orphans now—as many as half a million. Most of these orphans were homeless. Many had seen one or both of their parents killed, and many were disabled. I saw the pictures. Children without hands, children without feet. But their faces registered resignation, not self-pity. They were just going about the difficult business of surviving. Missing a limb, big deal: Who wasn't?

But why so many disabled *children*? Because of the land mines, I discovered. Afghan soil was permeated with them. It was worse there than anywhere else. The global land mine problem is widely publicized today, but back then, the issue was lost in the noise of all the other causes.

A dozen children a week were getting their limbs blown off, I learned, because children were more apt to pick up shiny things. And in the first decade of the war, I suddenly remembered, the Soviets had developed land mines that looked like small toys, specifically to attract children. Those mines were not very powerful. They didn't usually kill. They just took off a hand or an arm. And that was the point. Dead children don't cause much trouble for a population. They just get buried. But crippled children—ah! They become burdens on their families. Cripple enough children and you can bog down a whole population bent on guerrilla warfare. Good strategy! Someone probably got a promotion for coming up with that idea. I pictured my own little girl Elina . . . playing in our back yard, seeing something shiny. . . .

The UN had a program that cleared land mines, and I talked to some Afghan friends about raising some money for that program. We discussed producing an evening of Afghan music. But experienced American fund-raisers told me I was kidding myself. No one would donate to such a cause now. The only thing most people knew about

Afghans was that "they oppress women." Never mind that most Afghans *were* women. To the American public, Afghanistan equaled Taliban. Maybe if I denounced the Taliban up front, I might have a chance, I was told. Otherwise, women's groups might picket me.

But the Afghan community was divided on the Taliban issue. If we promoted our fund-raiser as an anti-Taliban rally, some Afghans would be angered. We would cause a blowup in the Afghan community. None of my Afghan friends wanted to stir up that kind of trouble. The land mine project fizzled.

Meanwhile, Help the Afghan Children had raised something like eight thousand dollars. They promised to apply it quickly to the needs of the half million disabled orphans. I remember that the big phenomenon that summer was the movie *The Blair Witch Project,* which attracted millions of visitors to a Web site that reported a fictional tragedy as if it were news. On TV, I saw a show about a suburban housewife who had her own sex Web site. She was getting good traffic—in the tens of thousands. When I logged on to Help the Afghan Children, I noticed I was visitor number 583.

When I think of the summer of 1999, I think of land mines, and of feeling helpless.

In August 2000, I went to New York with my older daughter, Jessamyn, to look at some colleges. One day, we had to get to Lincoln Center quickly, so we hailed a cab. I got into the front seat and Jessamyn got in back. The driver was muttering with road rage over some traffic incident, and I wanted to distract him, calm him down, get him in good spirits. So I struck up a conversation. Since he had an accent, I asked were he was from.

"Egypt," he said angrily.

"Are you really? Hey! I'm from Afghanistan." I stretched out my hand for a shake, expecting some light feeling of camaraderie.

But he didn't shake. He touched my sleeve suddenly, his air subtly and disturbingly reverent. "Afghanistan!" he muttered. "*You* are the *true* Muslims."

"Well," I demurred. "These days—"

"No," he insisted, "You are the ones living the pure Islam. Thank God for the Taliban. Now at last, God will help us to sweep away all this filth." And he waved in a broad gesture that took in all of New York around us. "I hate America," he uttered fervently. It took me aback. I've heard other people say, "I hate America," but once I heard it from this man, I knew that none of them had ever really meant it.

I wanted to establish at once that we were not compeers on this topic, so he could just stop sharing. "I feel pretty okay about America."

But the emotion swelling in him was too hard to contain. "Do you want to know what I hate about America?"

"No."

"The sluts," he blurted. "The booze. The filth."

I was intensely conscious of my daughter in the back seat.

"In Egypt," he confided, "I am a lawyer. I have a family. But I can't earn enough money to support them. I can make more money driving a cab here than being a lawyer there. So I come here six months a year. But I never bring my wife, even for a visit. I will never bring her! I don't want her to get polluted. One of my friends brought his wife here, and you know what she said to him? After she had been here for a few months, she said to him, 'Don't touch me anymore.'"

His knuckles went white on the steering wheel. This was the taxi ride I'd seen in the movies as comic relief, but I wasn't laughing.

Buckle your seat belt, because this gets worse.

"You know what I would do to my wife," he said, "if she ever said that to me?"

"This is our stop!"

"I would take her to the country—"

"You can drop us right here!"

"I would dig a hole—"

"Stop this cab!"

"I would put her in that hole . . ."

I heard nothing from Jessamyn in the back seat. Luckily, the guy was muttering his fantasy in a low voice, and she was lost in her own thoughts. I managed to get us out of that cab, and she never heard his rant. But my sleep was troubled that night. What worried me was the way he connected his own disturbed psyche to the Taliban phenomenon. Now that *they* were in the world, God would intervene in history and make sure his wife never refused him sex on demand—that seemed to be the equation.

In D.C. later that month, my cousin Farid told me of a Taliban practice: They punished women for supposed sexual impropriety by putting them in holes alive, burying them up to their necks, and leaving them to die.

Then he gave me a copy of a book about the Taliban by a Pakistani journalist, Ahmed Rashid. Nothing in the book was new to me, but everything in it chilled me. I already thought of the Taliban as an ignorant gang. Now I saw how they might serve as the keystone in an arch of ideas that seemed to me to have been taking shape in the Muslim world for the last twenty years. Ideas that had captured my brother's attention. Ideas I had heard described in that blue room in Morocco by the shopkeeper Abdullah. Ideas laid out rapturously by Abdul Qayum under that bare bulb in Istanbul. . . .

Ideas like the one that equates religion to a mechanism. Do all the practices just so and you create a smooth, well-oiled community. Get that community going, and God comes in like clockwork on your side. Then the apocalyptic showdown begins. And in that cosmic showdown, you could be the pivotal figure—yes, you, little man. Be proud, you angry little cabdriver whose wife won't sleep with you—your anguish is not personal; it's historical. Her defiance doesn't mean you're creepy; no need to take another look at yourself and your behavior. It means she's in the clutches of Satan. Conquering her is firing a shot for God.

I had thought of the Taliban as terrible for Afghanistan. Now, suddenly, I saw them as a potential menace far beyond their borders. They couldn't be discounted, because their story did reflect certain themes of Islamic thought and history. The early miracles of Islam did include the political fact of the first community. A tiny band of Bedouins living a crude life in an arid wasteland laid low both the superpowers of their time, the Sassanids and the Byzantines. How could they possibly have done this? God must have helped them.

And what had the Taliban done so far? Toppled the Soviet empire. At least so went their mystique. One superpower down, one to go. It didn't matter that it wasn't really them but their mujahideen forebears and a combination of historical forces—the Taliban believed it of themselves, and apparently so did millions of embittered Muslims around the world. And what did the Taliban proclaim as their mission? To establish a community in which the exact practices of seventh-century Medina were duplicated. The pure Islamic state that the Abdullahs and the Abdul Qayums and the angry cabdrivers of the world were waiting for.

I worried about the Taliban not as a military force but as an idea. Their power, it struck me, lay not in their guns but in their beards. I brought this worry home with me from my trip to the East Coast that summer.

One year and one month later, a handful of madmen hijacked two airliners and flew them into the twin towers of the World Trade Center.

EPILOGUE

Growing up bicultural is like straddling a crack in the earth. If the cultures are far apart— like those of Afghanistan and America—one feels an urge to get entirely over to one side or the other. My siblings and I grew up with such divided souls, and we responded in different ways.

Rebecca shifted almost entirely to the West, even though she was born in the lost world at its most intact and spent the most years in Afghanistan. After college, she married a conservative business professor named Bob Pettys, who appreciated her American persona and took no interest in her exotic origins, not even in Afghan food—fried chicken was just fine. And with a name like Rebecca Pettys, new acquaintances were never moved to say, "Hmm. Interesting name. Where are you from?"

She got a Ph.D. in theater, and although she wrote her

dissertation on Iranian religious passion plays, she never taught a course in that subject. She and her husband ended up at a small college in the South, where no Afghans were likely to ever wander through. There, she focused on the classic curriculum of Western theater and on mounting shows drawn from the standard English and American repertoire, with an occasional Greek tragedy thrown in. As for Farsi, she virtually never spoke it again. To her, the East came to mean New York.

Riaz had the least Afghanistan in him: He never experienced the lost world, he lived the fewest years in Afghanistan, and six of those years were spent in American Lashkargah, where he didn't even go to an Afghan school, as we older siblings did. Yet he shifted to the East as thoroughly as he was able. He couldn't become culturally Afghan, because that's not something to which you can convert; the only way to become Afghan is to bury yourself in the culture and grow an Afghan self. Riaz had no access to such soil, so he grasped what he could, the Islam part, especially those aspects available from texts.

He eventually left America altogether and moved to Dubai, one of the United Arab Emirates, and there he lives today, teaching Arabic to the numerous Africans, Asians, and other non-Arabs flowing through, and translating Arabic texts into English for a religious publishing house. My father saw Riaz in Delhi a few weeks after his conversion, and upon returning to Afghanistan he told the cousins, "I'm glad my boy has become devout, but . . . he goes a bit too far." In other words, Riaz's soul ended up even east of Kabul—somewhere in that wasp's nest of Islamic enthusiasm called Pakistan.

I, on the other hand, tried to straddle the fault line, although, to be sure, I shifted my weight quite definitely over to my American foot. If Afghanistan were to vanish from my life, I wouldn't fall over. Yet I've always managed to keep one foot touching down on the other side of the line. I've never stopped reading and writing about Afghanistan and Islam. I've kept up Afghan friendships and connections to my Afghan relatives. I still speak decent Farsi, I translate poetry from that language, and I cook a mean Afghan meal.

And I wonder why. Why won't my soul let go? It's not really comfortable to be bicultural; I can attest to that. Among Afghans, I've always felt allowances being made for my American side, as if it's a sort of disability. My American self makes me a little less Afghan. Thus, along with the undeniable pleasure I get from speaking Farsi and socializing with others of my original culture, I always feel like an outsider in a way that I never could if I were truly an outsider—because in the latter case, I would be a tourist instead of a misfit.

When my center of gravity shifted to America, I didn't know Afghanistan was going to be consumed in a twenty-three-year holocaust. That's not why I drifted to this side. It was more that being an Afghan among Americans made me no less American. After all, most Americans are something else, as well. America's characteristic flavor is made of the otherness we all bring to this stew. Also, individualism is at the heart of being an American. We like to think of all our group affiliations as voluntary. We're 200 million people, all of whom fancy themselves unique—different. And maybe many of us are deluding ourselves; maybe we're just cookie-stamped figures in a faceless crowd. But the point is that we try to be unique; we honor that enterprise. And *different* was an inescapable part of my identity from the start, so I gravitated to the one place where *different* didn't mean *suspect.*

But why, then, did I not let go of Afghanistan the way Rebecca did?

I don't know, but whatever shape-shifting my narrative has gone through, the accident of history that gave me a divided soul has always been the original fact. It planted in me a troubled sense of duty that has never ceased to nag. I always felt I was supposed to do something with this peculiarity of mine, use it for some purpose. I was always searching the horizon for some sign of this work. Was I to write the great Afghan-American novel? Form a delegation to . . . ? Raise money to . . . ?

And while I stood contemplating the horizon, terrorists attacked New York, and I wrote a little e-mail, and a screaming cacophony of noise and light burst through my life. When the tumult moved on and I picked myself up and looked back, I realized that was it—the thing I had been searching the horizon for all my life: It was in the past now. It was the e-mail. In those twenty minutes of outpour, some of the current bolting between East and West passed through the infinitesimal circuit of my life. I spoke for Afghanistan with my American voice, and while I was writing, my two selves were fused. Aside from some facility with words, what I brought to that moment was the mere fact that fifty-six years ago, my mother and father fell in love.

Two months after the attacks, a newsman asked me to collect some Afghans for a televised roundtable discussion. I shook the tree of my Afghan connections and came up with an interesting cast. It included pink-faced Abdul Hudood Zafari, who ran the Helmand Valley Authority after our time and held an office in the Afghan Communist government before defecting. It included hawk-faced Majid Mansoury, who, after twenty years in America, happened to visit Kabul just when the warlords were driving out the Communists. Majid ended up serving in the warlord government for four years, even though he had a wife and children and a life back in America.

Also with us was shy Shakila Omar, a woman who was busy building a Web site and organizing a foundation to keep alive the memory of Ahmed Shah Massoud. Then there was Daoud Wahab, who spent two years in Afghanistan during the Taliban era as an aide-de-camp to Massoud. He had been in charge of hospitality for visiting dignitaries, and he had arranged housing for the two affable Arab journalists who assassinated Massoud the next morning by blowing themselves up in his presence. Rounding out our cast was Khaled Hosseini, a young

Afghan doctor whose passion after work was writing—not *ghazals*, not *quasidas*, not even *rubaiyat*, but horror stories in the tradition of H. P. Lovecraft.

My cousins Zahir and Shafiqa agreed to host the event. Shafiqa put together the usual mountainous feast in preparation for the camera crew. The crew members were scheduled to arrive at two o'clock, but at 1:55 they called to tell us they had stumbled across a better Afghanistan story on the way to our house and would not be coming after all.

Undoubtedly, the media will find a better story than Afghanistan itself in days to come, and the land of my father will again slip into obscurity. But that day, anyway, it didn't matter. At least my fellow Afghans graciously assured me that it didn't matter; it was enough that the eight of us got to meet one another and share our stories. We ate sugar-coated almonds and pistachio-flavored candies and drank tea, just like in the old country. Oddly, though, I did not feel myself slipping into my Afghan self for this occasion. Somehow, this group didn't raise the question of Afghan self or American self. In their own ways, all these Afghans had selves as fractured as mine. The world is full of such Afghans now, as I've learned since September 11. Afghanistan itself, or at least the one I knew, is like a glass vase pounded by rocks for twenty-three years. For all of us, surrendering to diversity is probably the only plausible path left to attaining unity. The international community is supposedly committed to helping the country rebuild, but the lost world will not be reconstituted. Whatever rises from the rubble will be something new, and I suspect I may not have to decide who I am in order to take some part in this impending Afghanistan, because I am a kaleidoscope of parts now—and so is Afghanistan. So is the world, when you get right down to it.

The E-mail

DEAR FRIENDS—

I've been hearing a lot of talk about "bombing Afghanistan back to the Stone Age." One radio talk-show host allowed that this would mean killing innocent people, people who had nothing to do with this atrocity, but "we're at war, we have to accept collateral damage. What else can we do?"

Minutes later I heard some TV pundit discussing whether we "have the belly to do what must be done."

And I thought about the issues being raised especially hard because I am from Afghanistan, and even though I've lived here for thirty-five years, I've never lost track of what's going on there. So I want to tell anyone who will listen how it all looks from where I'm standing.

I speak as one who hates the Taliban and Osama Bin Laden. There is no doubt in my mind that these people were responsible for the atrocity in New York. I agree that something must be done about those monsters.

But the Taliban and Bin Laden are not Afghanistan. They're not even the government of Afghanistan. The Taliban are a cult of ignorant psychotics who took over Afghanistan in 1997. Bin Laden is a political criminal with a plan.

When you think "Taliban," think "Nazis." When you think "Bin Laden," think "Hitler." And when you think "the people of Afghanistan," think "the Jews in the concentration camps."

It's not only that the Afghan people had nothing to do with this atrocity. They were the first victims of the perpetrators. They would exult if someone would come in there, take out the Taliban, and clear out the rat's nest of international thugs holed up in their country.

Some say, Why don't the Afghans rise up and overthrow the Taliban? The answer is, They're starved, exhausted, hurt, incapacitated, suffering. A few years ago, the United Nations estimated that there are 500,000 disabled orphans in Afghanistan—a country with no economy, no food. There are millions of widows. And the Taliban has been burying these widows alive in mass graves. The soil is littered with land mines, the farms were all destroyed by the Soviets. These are a few of the reasons why the Afghan people have not overthrown the Taliban.

We come now to the question of bombing Afghanistan

back to the Stone Age. Trouble is, that's been done. The Soviets took care of it already.

Make the Afghans suffer? They're already suffering. Level their houses? Done. Turn their schools into piles of rubble? Done. Eradicate their hospitals? Done. Destroy their infrastructure? Cut them off from medicine and health care? Too late. Someone already did all that.

New bombs would only stir the rubble of earlier bombs. Would they at least get the Taliban? Not likely. In today's Afghanistan, only the Taliban eat, only they have the means to move around. They'd slip away and hide.

Maybe the bombs would get some of those disabled orphans—they don't move too fast, they don't even have wheelchairs. But flying over Kabul and dropping bombs wouldn't really be a strike against the criminals who did this horrific thing. Actually, it would only be making common cause with the Taliban—by raping once again the people they've been raping all this time.

So what else is there? What can be done, then? Let me now speak with true fear and trembling. The only way to get Bin Laden is to go in there with ground troops. When people speak of "having the belly to do what needs to be done," they're thinking in terms of having the belly to kill as many as needed, having the belly to overcome any moral qualms about killing innocent people. Let's pull our heads out of the sand. What's actually on the table is Americans dying. And not just because some Americans would die fighting their way through Afghanistan to Bin Laden's hideout. It's much bigger than that, folks. Because to get any troops to Afghanistan, we'd have to go through Pakistan. Would they let us?

Not likely. The conquest of Pakistan would have to be first. Will other Muslim nations just stand by? You see where I'm going. We're flirting with a world war between Islam and the West.

And guess what: That's Bin Laden's program. That's exactly what he wants. That's why he did this. Read his speeches and statements. It's all right there. He really believes Islam would beat the West. It might seem ridiculous, but he figures if he can polarize the world into Islam and the West, he's got a billion soldiers. If the West wreaks a holocaust in those lands, that's a billion people with nothing left to lose, and that's even better, from Bin Laden's point of view. He's probably wrong: In the end the West would win, whatever that would mean, but the war would last for years and millions would die, not just theirs but ours. Who has the belly for that?

Bin Laden does. Anyone else?

TAMIM ANSARY

ACKNOWLEDGMENTS

Thanks to my wife, Deborah Krant, for listening to troublesome chapters first; to all my friends at the San Francisco Writer's Workshop for feedback; to Farid, Zahir, Shafiqa, and Wahid Ansary for information; and to the people who received my e-mail about Afghanistan and apparently passed it on: Gary Turchin, Susan Hoffman, Toivo Kallas, Debbie Faigenbaum, Kip Knox, Lisa Schuchman, Erika Mailman, Joe Quirk, Teya Penniman, Tom Williamson, Rick Schmidt, Larry Beresford, Mike Carroll, Margaret Kitchell, Julie Castiglia, Steve Feinstein, Sandra Mangurian, and Dale Martin. Special thanks also to Paul Elie, my patient editor, and Julia Castiglia, my tireless agent.